UK Haunted Hospitality
Volume 3:
Eateries

- Dr Paul Lee -

Copyright 2025 -

By the same author

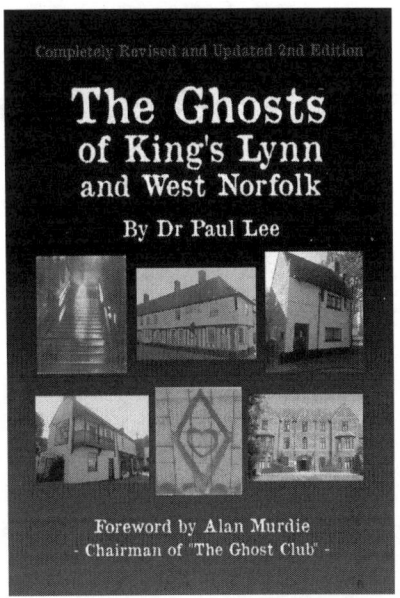

Completely Revised and Updated 2nd Edition

The Ghosts
of King's Lynn
and West Norfolk

By Dr Paul Lee

Foreword by Alan Murdie
- Chairman of "The Ghost Club" -

**UK
Haunted
Hospitality**

Volume 1:
Pubs and Clubs

by Dr Paul Lee

**UK
Haunted
Hospitality**

Volume 2:
Hotels and other
accommodation

by Dr Paul Lee

Contents

Introduction

Welcome to the third edition of "UK Haunted Hospitality," covering haunted restaurants, coffee shops, tea rooms and other similar eatery establishments (including such oddities as a milk bar in an old spectrally infested location!)

This volume is obviously much smaller than its predecessors; the most obvious reason is that there are comparatively fewer dedicated "eateries" than pubs or hotels, but, as noted in volume 1, it proved to be extremely difficult to differentiate between pubs and restaurants – and many establishments use the phrase "gastropub" which blurs the distinction between purely drinking and purely eating venues. One Scottish chain lists all its pubs as "restaurants" which obviously doesn't help! Naturally, some mistakes will have been made and for this I offer many apologies.

Because of the lack of locations, the maps have been grouped together not by county, but by region (South East, West Midlands and so on).

As was performed in volumes 1 and 2, a mini survey of all the venues listed was conducted (a few establishments were found to have closed since the last survey a few years back) but this was met with a disappointing lack of responses. A number of places were also contacted based on speculation as there had been ghost reports in neighbouring premises or in the immediate vicinity; to no avail sadly. In the first few months of 2025 this author contacted all the major companies (both head office and relevant individual branches) to ascertain if anything ghostly had been reported. As can be appreciated this involved many dozens of emails and messages and the response was discouraging. Only one replied, and their suggestion was to contact branches individually, a completely implausible suggestion as there were several hundred such places nationwide!

Most of the venues are in England, and none in Northern Ireland or Wales; apologies for any disappointment in this regard. Scotland looked slightly more promising, but with a disappointingly low tally of 5 venues. A check of these showed that three had not only closed but their old premises were now empty and devoid of any activity (both from a ghostly and consumer point of view!)

If you have any further information on these or other venues, please contact me at paul@paullee.com and I will include them on the updates page on my website.

Paul Lee

October 2025

The use of letters inside square brackets after the name denotes whether the establishment is a restaurant ('[R]') or a tea room/coffee shop/cafe (['T']), although sometimes the determination was not easy!

Page numbers for the locations are denoted by the numerals under the icons on the maps.

As one appreciates, the function of venues is fluid and sometimes the establishments listed in this book were not always dedicated to the provision of food or drink in the past; and one might expect that phenomena were reported in a building's old guise, as well as possibly its current incarnation. It may be that the ghosts are now dormant, extinct, or were person- rather than location-centric and followed an unfortunate individual when they moved on. There could, therefore, be nothing to inflict ghostly mayhem at present.

For this reason, the building's old identity and purpose (if known) has been indicated in italics and is preceded by an asterisk, if phenomena was noted *there*. Sometimes, but not always, the spectral activity has "spilled over" into the current premises and if so, this is included in the italicised list of names. If not, this usually indicates that no data exists for the present address and occupiers.

If there are no italicised entries, then this may indicate that paranormal activity is still in evidence in the current property; but given the lack of response from the proprietors it is impossible to know.

Updates and details of newly discovered ghostly eateries can be found on the author's website :
http://www.paullee.com/geatery

South West

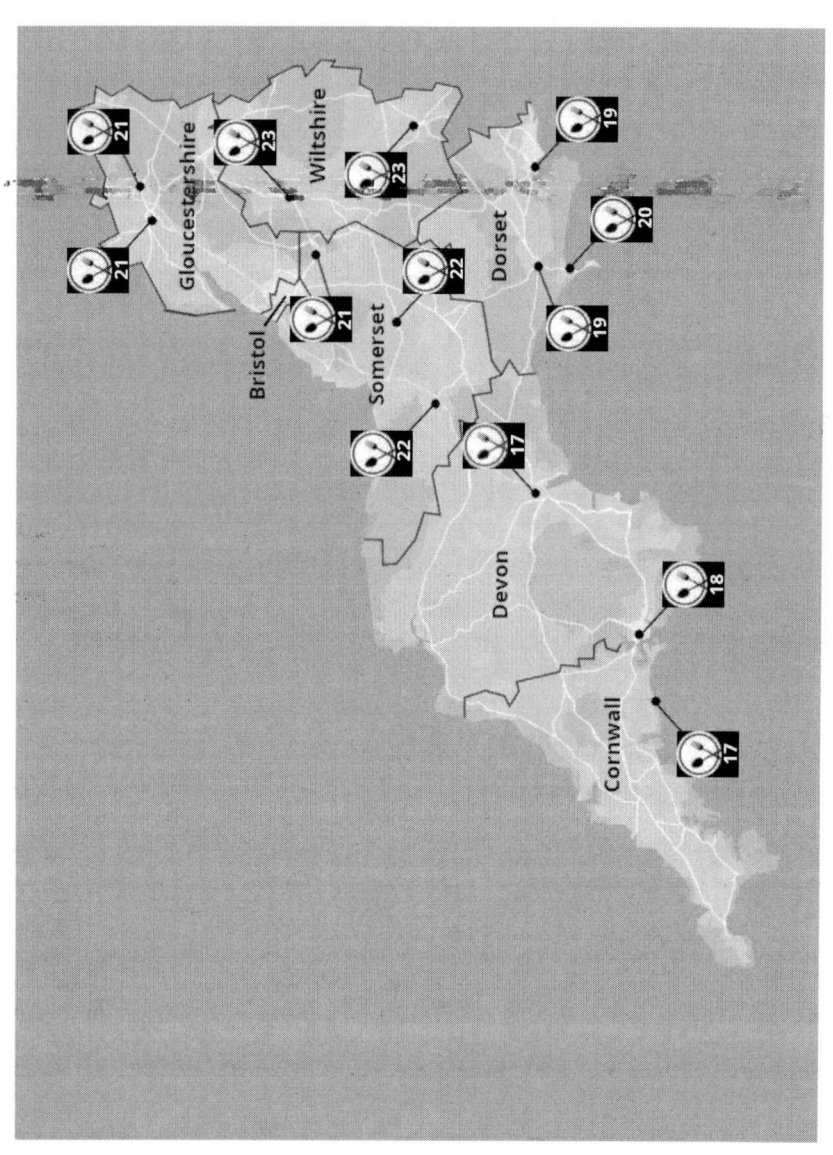

Cornwall

Looe

The Golden Guinea [R]
Fore Street, The Quay, PL13 1AD

A figure, wearing 17th century clothing consisting of a dark frock coat and white leggings has been seen inside the establishment as well as in the street outside. Groans and loud creaks have been heard in the building too.

Smugglers Cott [R]
Middle Market Street, The Quay, Looe PL13 1AY

A pale girl wearing rags has been seen on the stairs, while there is "a dark figure" in the secret smuggling tunnel to the quay and adjoining room, now a part of the restaurant, and which was unearthed in the 1930s. This latter phantom is said to be boisterous and throws items around the establishment.

Devon

Exeter

Eat On The Green [R]   *Hanson's Tea room
2 Cathedral Close, EX1 1EZ

Under previous owners, an employee saw a bizarre sight in the premises; a ghostly lady - but only her bottom half was visible. The phantom passed through a wall, prompting the member to staff to flee the building. She never returned to her job. There had also been incidents of items temporarily vanishing and being found in odd places, and poltergeist-like pranks, like piles of plates left in the sink crashing to the floor.

Pizza Express [R]   *Tinley's tea room/Pizza Express
2, Broadgate, Cathedral Yard, EX1 1HJ

Parts of this building date back to the 16th century which may help explain its spectral heritage; certainly, sightings date back several decades at least. For instance, when the building was occupied by Tinley's tearooms, four ghostly monks were seen in the winter of 1982 warming themselves

17

around a long disused fireplace; a more recent spectre has been described as wearing an "ancient costume." He sits in the restaurant and then gets up and walks down to the cellar, where staff cannot locate him. There are also stories of "Percy Poltergeist" plaguing the building with footsteps, tappings, tables being moved and interference with the music system including yanking the plug out of the wall. A legend talks of one of the phantoms being the spectre of "Old Friendly Fred" who allegedly was executed for failing in his duty to secure the adjacent Broadgate, which was demolished in 1824/5. With the gate to the Cathedral open an unknown assailant entered and murdered a member of the clergy. The flat above the restaurant has (or had) played host to some bizarre experiences, including bulbs and clothing going missing, a heavy bookcase being pushed over, cold spots and a knife being flung across a room.

Richies South Indian Restaurant [R] *The Conservatory restaurant*
18 North Street, EX4 3QS
A man has been seen outside the building staring at it and shaking his head as if displaying his disapproval. It is said that he is a former owner, when the premises was a dwelling.

Plymouth

Kapadokya Restaurant [R]   *Shirley Valentine's Taverna/Kapadokya*
12 New Street, PL1 2NA
This building is said to date to the 16th century and has had a few ghostly phenomena experienced; under previous owners, there had been a few incidents reported comprising unexplained footsteps, glimpses of a person's head or outline descending the stairs, a woman observed standing in the upstairs area and items falling from a windowsill.
The current occupier told me in May 2023 that there were still ongoing reports of noises and shadow figures. No more details could be obtained.

Tudor Rose Tearoom [T]
36 New Street, PL1 2NA
Another 16th century building in this, the oldest street in Plymouth. Historical reports talked of footsteps being heard and figures seen on the first floor, which was vacant at the time. Another ghost, an elderly lady, was reputed to have some sentience. She was seen in the corner of the tea room

and even spoke to people. There have been a few incidents of poltergeist pranks; in one incident, a cake was hurled off the counter after a customer had ordered it.

The tea room would still seem to have some activity. The owner told me in January 2020 that while she had never experienced anything herself, a lot of people had. She said that these included an old lady (some say she wears blue) and children; all of them were reported to be very friendly. In March 2025 it was confirmed that the Blue Lady was still in evidence in the banquet room, seen most regularly by customers (but not sadly by my correspondent). There is also a "vortex" on the staircase and a poltergeist that moved an object back to its original position. My contact was quite grateful that she doesn't see the ghosts and doesn't take their non appearance as a slight; "I speak to them sometimes and ask them to not show their presence to me because I do not wish to be afraid. I have never experienced any negative vibes in the place."

Dorset

Dorchester

Al Molo Dorchester [R] *Judge Jeffreys Restaurant*
6 High West Street, DT1 1UJ

There would seem to have been a structure located here since 1270 when it was owned by the Monastery at Abbotsbury but its most famous occupant was the "Hanging Judge" George Jeffreys who used the premises as his lodges during the 1685 Bloody Assizes. The building, many centuries later, adopted the name of its famous occupant when it was a restaurant and there are claims that people saw him staring out of the window into the street; other elements of phantom mischief such as objects moving and footsteps and banging noises were blamed on the late Judge's phantom. Incidentally, when the building was undergoing renovation work in 1928, human bones were discovered behind a wall in the courtyard. The bone's identity remains a mystery.

In March 2025, the current proprietor informed me that they had been here for 3 years (and lived in the building for 2½ of those years) and had experienced nothing - "not a knock or a bump or anything."

Poole

The Customs House [T] *?
The Quay, BH15 1HJ

Replacing a building that was destroyed by fire and dating to 1813, this establishment was used for the collection of taxes from vessels entering the harbour. A "dark man," said to be a smuggler, haunts the top floor and is believed to be a man named Carter, who it is said informed the authorities of the identities of his fellow compatriots who would retrieve their cargo of smuggled tea from the House at night. For his treachery, Carter was stoned and drowned by his comrades. Nearby on the quayside, Captain Johnson's ghost, wearing a dark coat and wide-brimmed hat has been observed; in life, he was in charge of seizing smuggled goods.

In January 2020, the customs house replied to my query about any recent phenomena. They said that since they took over in 2018 they have experienced nothing. This was confirmed in a follow-up email five years later (note that the restaurant does not seem to occupy the area where "Carter" has been seen in the past)

Oriel Restaurant [R]
aka Oriel On The Quay
Seaway House, The Quay, BH15 1HJ

An old man with a long grey beard and a cloth cap has been sitting in the corner. He has been identified as an elderly sailor (the building was a chapel for sea men operated by the Mission of Seafarers charity prior to the restaurant opening in 1955). Meanwhile on the second floor, heavy footsteps and coughing has been heard.

Weymouth

By The Quay [T]   *Seagull Cafe*
10 Trinity Street, DT4 8TW

Although rarely seen, a ghostly old man was seen seated at table No.2 and liked to sprinkle salt on the surface; he was also prone to pranks and startled the ex-owner's wife by saying "Boo!" behind her, as well as patting her and blowing in her ear.

The current owners told me in March 2025 that they had recently been experiencing some things they had found unusual. But when clarification was sought on this tantalising snippet, I was told that nothing had happened that was unexplainable and that the new and fresh 'vibe' "takes up the space."

Gloucestershire

Cheltenham

The Ivy Montpellier Brasserie [R]   *Lloyd's Bank*
Montpellier Walk, GL50 1SW
Unfortunately details are lacking except that bank workers would experience "strange happenings."
There would seem to be a total absence of activity at the building since it became a restaurant according to staff in July 2021.

Gloucester

Coffee #1 [T]   *travel agent/Kendall's Fashion Store/Next*
25 Northgate Street, GL1 2AN
The previous occupants of this building have all had brushes with unexplained phenomena; the stockroom was reported as being cold, hangers would be shaken and the hair of shop assistants would be pulled "playfully." When staff unlocked in the morning, they found that items had been moved overnight, and they would also experience pungent smells and cold rushes of air. The only report of an apparition, nicknamed "Fred" described him as being grey and five feet tall.

Somerset

Bath

Amarone Restaurant [R] *Popjoy/The Strada*

Beau Nash House, Saw Close BA1 1EU

Beau Nash, "The Master of Ceremonies" in Bath lived here with his mistress Juliana Popjoy and it is she who has returned in death to her old home. She has/had been seen in the upstairs reception room, while another (?) lady phantom has been seen dining alone but when approached she fades from sight.

Rui [R] *The Crown Inn*
23 Bathwick Street, BA2 6NY

The spectre of a man dressed in the uniform of a First World War soldier drinking ale from a tankard was seen.

Glastonbury

Coffee Zero [T]
42 High Street, BA6 9DX

Pauline Plant informed me of this location and was told of several "unnerving" incidents from a member of staff. On one occasion as the employee entered the premises after opening up, she was greeted by a voice saying "Hello." There was no one else in the building and she was so perturbed that she wouldn't re-enter until a colleague arrived. Random and unexplained knocks occur regularly and the back of the premises is said to be the most active area, and there is the feeling of a presence in the 'wash room' which is also unusually cold. Another time, a six pack of blue kitchen rolls flew off the shelf in the storeroom. Alas, her boss was not entirely sympathetic to these incidents of spectral torment and simply laughed at her.

Taunton

Caffe Nero [T]
15 Fore Street, TA1 1HX

Another building with claimed sightings of the wraith of Judge Jeffreys, it is said that he either stayed here, or was entertained to dinner in 1685.

Wiltshire

Chippenham

La Vecchia Orsa [R]   *The Bear Hotel*
12 Market Place, SN15 3HJ
    It is not known if the ghosts are still encountered as the current restaurant occupies the ground floor and most of the phantoms were noted on upper storeys. But in the past, a woman in grey was seen to open an upper window and lean out but when the room was checked, it was empty and the window was still fastened shut. Voices were also heard coming from a bedroom, but again, it was found to be empty when checked; on another occasion, a housekeeper walking to the hotel saw a grey lady close the curtains in this same room but it was found to be unoccupied that day. The cellar door was known to open to reveal a figure, sometimes accompanied by footsteps. It is also in the cellar that the landlord at the time felt something thrown at him.

Salisbury

Rai d'Or [R]
69 Brown Street, SP1 2AS
    Unfortunately there are few details of this establishment's five ghosts, other than one is called "The Doctor" and is seen by the fireplace. However, all of the spectres are claimed to be friendly.

South East
(including London)

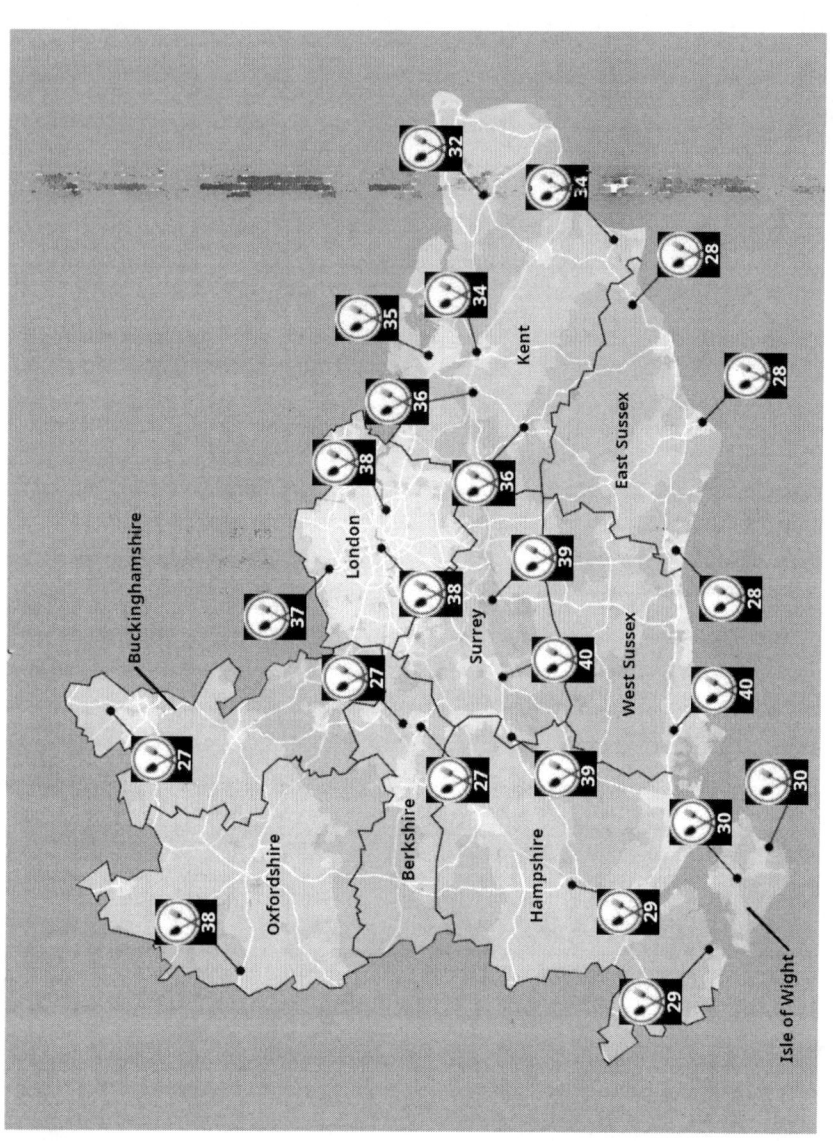

Berkshire

Bracknell

The Horse And Groom Harvester [R]
Bagshot Road, RG12 9RB

The mischievous spirit likes to help itself to a few drops from the spirit (!) cupboard.

Warfield

The Spice Lounge at The Three Legged Cross [R]
Forest Road, RG42 6AE

Over a hundred years ago a gypsy woman was barred from the hostelry and placed a curse on pub and its landlord, who soon passed away. It is reputed that the gypsy haunts the outside of the building but it was noted in 2021 that "No new hauntings have been recorded however."

Buckinghamshire

Newport Pagnell

Pin Petch [R]   *Odell and Co Ltd Ironmongers*
13 High Street, MK16 8AR

The ghost of a girl called Emily who burned to death is said to haunt numbers 11 and 13; at some point in the past it is reputed that she used to cook breakfasts for workmen at No.11 and died when her apron caught fire. Occupants of Odell's have smelt food cooking when they opened in the morning and have found items moved overnight. A staff member passing through the cellar on his way to the toilets was perturbed when he felt something which he likened to being walked across. It is also in the cellar that another staff member heard a banging noise issuing from upstairs; when he ascended the stairs although there was no one to be seen, items could still be seen swaying from the reverberations. It is also on the ground floor that a figure was seen inside the locked up building at night but there was no intruder upon investigation. Other phenomena include tools and other items being found on the floor after being dislodged from their hooks, the burglar alarm sounding in the night, a lady's face appearing on the tiles, and a calendar swinging by itself. It is said that, of 2011 anyway, the property is "quiet" of ghostly misdemeanours.

East Sussex

Brighton

Pearly Cow Brighton [R] *The Fisherman's Rest pub*
123 Kings Road, BN1 2FA
"Strange, indistinct shapes" had been seen on CCTV and people experienced "sudden icy chills."

Eastbourne

The Tally Ho [R]
42 Church Street, Old Town, BN21 1BJ
Although rarely observed, a girl had been heard talking in various areas of the restaurant and is described as "happy." In one incident she surprised a woman by tapping her on the shoulder.
In January 2020, the owners told me that in their 6 years of residency, they had experienced nothing in that time.

Rye

Fletchers House [T]
2 Lion Street, TN31 7LB

Frequently heard are the sounds of footsteps ascending the stairs; there is also a tall young man in a suit but his apparition is rarely seen.

The Union Rye [R]
8 East Street, TN31 7JY
There are a number of apparitions in this establishment; there is a solid-looking blonde girl in a white dress who walks through the restaurant towards the kitchen at which point she vanishes. There may be another ghostly girl, said to be 16-18 years old in a long red dress who has been seen in more recent years. A large man, possibly that of a seaman, has been observed walking through a bedroom doorway to look out of a window whereupon he then retraces his steps. Poltergeist-like pranks have also been noted; cold spots, the feeling of being touched, pinched and slapped and a door that has opened by itself and then slammed shut have all been noted here too.

The restaurant would appear to be quiet at present; an employee told me in July 2021, "I'm afraid nothing of interest with regards to odd or inexplicable phenomena."

Hampshire

Lymington

The Ferryman [R]
Undershore Road, SO41 5SB
This building dates back to the 1600s, but its ghostly heritage seems to date back to 1893 when it was known as "The Waggon and Horses." A sign by the door in the current pub describes the "Ardlamont Shooting Case," where a Lieutenant Dudley Cecil Hambrough was found shot in the head from behind and there was speculation that he might have done it himself. On September 5th 1893, local gamekeeper Henry Card walked into the tap room of this pub with his shotgun and elected to show to John Bligh, a visitor from London, how it was possible for someone to accidentally discharge a gun from behind while carrying it. Tragically, Card was mistaken in his belief that

his own weapon was empty and during his "experiment" he received a fatal wound to the head; his ghost is still said to walk the premises.

Over the years, the story has become garbled, with the initial incident being linked not to Hambrough, but a local farmer, found dead in his field. He had no known enemies and suicide seemed unlikely.

Winchester

ASK Italian [R]
God Begot House, 101 High Street, SO23 9AH

The current building dates to 1050 (although at least one source puts its date as 1462, the difference in years possibly due to the alterations and extra building work in intervening centuries). About a hundred years ago, while being converted from a bookshop to a hotel, a number of human bones, thought to have come from a Saxon cemetery were unearthed. The drawing room of the hotel was subject to unexplained rappings and dogs would not enter the room. An exorcism and further remodelling may have expelled the strange forces but literature in 2011 noted that strange crashing noises had been heard in the cellar.

There would, however, be more to the hauntings as the current manager told the press in late 2021. He said that if you were here on your own, you would hear stuff and get the feeling that there is someone there. His employees have heard whispers in their ears while on the stairs and a cleaner had her hair pulled while she was alone. Music turned itself on and off and a helium balloon that had left upstairs overnight followed the cleaner down the stairs and headed towards the kitchen. A little girl seated at a table felt someone invisible hold her hand and at the same table, a menu lifted of its own accord before falling to the floor. The manager said that 80% of the incidents occurred upstairs but nothing harmful happened but just enough to let people know that ... whatever ... was present.

Isle of Wight

Newport:

God's Providence [R]
12 St Thomas' Square,   PO30 1SL

The unusual name of this building, which was rebuilt as a private home in 1801 but still has elements of its original 1524 construction, derives from the story that the original building was the only place in Newport where no-one was afflicted by the plague in 1583. A little girl has been seen in "The Gift Room," and people here have felt the sensation of being touched lightly.

The tearoom told me in August 2021 that in the last 11 years of the current owner's stewardship, there had been a couple of new occurrences. An employee had her ear flicked forcibly when she was passing the small area between the kitchen and front of house areas. There was no-one else nearby at the time. My correspondent also told me that someone whispered her name loudly right in her ear. Again, she was alone and all the windows were shut. However, these incidents would seem to be a rarity; as I was told, "[The] last occurrence that actually holds water in my opinion was the waitress having her ear flicked and this was in late 2018."

Richmonds Cake & Coffee Co [T] *Jessop's camera store*
95-96 St James' Street, PO30 1HY

Previously, there were problems with the electrical supply in the building, and burglar alarms would activate for no reason. There were also incidents of footsteps, hammering on the front door, doors opening and closing, and four very heavy skips being found dragged across an upstairs room. It normally took two people to move them.

Shanklin

Paramount Cafe [T]
74 High Street, PO37 6NJ

The resident wraith is said to be "Charlie" who was an employee here many years ago. He is described as being between 45 and 55 with dark hair and piercing eyes. His most unusual manifestation was when he was seen asleep on a chair in the lounge, snoring! He vanished when the curtains were thrown open. He has been blamed for cold spots, footsteps, knives and utensils in the kitchen going missing (they eventually reappear), rattling of doors, the sounds of someone moving downstairs during the night, coffee and oranges being found spilt on the floor overnight and bulbs constantly blowing on the stairs.

The property replied to an email in February 2020 when I asked about any recent phenomena. The correspondent told me that although nothing had happened to him, things like pens, spray bottles, knives, menu pads, and utensils go missing but turn up again, sometimes months later. Five years later in March 2025, the owner told me that things still disappeared but reappeared again. Interestingly, he added that such incidents were sporadic and "might not happen for ages" - the last such occurrence was perhaps 6 months previously.

Vernon Cottage [R]
1 Eastcliff Road, PO37 6AA

The cottage dates to 1817, and the restaurant's website notes that the building was at "the very heart of the Island's smuggling operations in the early 19th century" and features a room where contraband could be concealed. The website also notes that the cottage is home to a beautiful enchanting female ghost called Frances, who was the housekeeper for 30 years. She fell in love with the original master of the house but died when she fell down the stairs. We are told, "Frances, who appears as her stunning younger self loves Vernon Cottage and leaves 5 pence pieces for the owners - and visitors - when she approves of their behaviour!" Other documentation talks of another (?) ghostly young girl who has been seen running from this restaurant down the lane where she meets a young man whereupon they both vanish.

Kent

Canterbury

Cafe Chambers [R]
59 Palace Street, CT1 2DY

A figure wearing a black and white striped jersey and identified as a seaman is to be seen near the first floor toilets, and his tobacco smoke detected too. There is also a phantom cat which has been heard in the rooms above the cafe.

In February 2020 the cafe replied to my query about any recent phenomena and said that they had not experienced anything in their 16 years of ownership but they did say that the building has "a wonderful feeling." However, staff had seen "the phantom" many times and had given him the nickname "George." In subsequent emails, the owner of the cafe elaborated: "Apparently he's a sailor of some sort, who wears overalls and a sailors cap, maybe a labourer. A really good friend of mine who used to work for me came down one night after she locked up and saw him standing at the counter, she thought it was a customer that she had locked in. When she turned around again to ask him what he wanted, he'd gone." Other than this, there had been other incidents, like the washing going missing.

Caffe Nero [T]
44 High Street, CT1 2SA
The building houses Queen Elizabeth's Guest Chamber, which is a single large room on the first floor; it is said that the titular monarch stayed here for her 40th birthday in 1573 although it is much more likely that she lodged at the Archbishop's Palace. When the building was a fruit shop, a young child would be seen tapping at the upstairs window despite this area being empty. During conversion work into a coffee shop, items were found on the old staircase over several weeks, ranging to a collection of silver coins dating to the 13th century to a child's shoe from the 1600s. This is despite the building being secured every night. Employees of the coffee shop have felt cold spots on different floors within the building.

The Cosy Club [R] *Waterstones
20-21 St Margaret's Street, CT1 2TH
Elise, a nanny who fell three flights down the stairs and died, has been blamed for doors slamming at the rear of the premises when it housed a book shop, and tea and coffee pots rattling in the top floor cafe. People have also detected a drop in temperature and perfume, and books went missing, or been found re-arranged in the basement book store (this is where the remains of a Roman Bath House can still be seen through a panel in the wall.)

Tiny Tim's Tearoom [T]
34 St Margaret's Street, CT1 2TG
In 1964 the building housed a Chinese restaurant but a suspicious fire in 1986 reduced the building to little more than ruins. The Kent Archaeological Society website talks of what was found during refurbishment; "Within the walls of the attic were the mummified bodies of three children, all clutching bibles inscribed with the date 1503. Alongside

these were mummified cats and dogs, thought to have been placed earlier than the children to ward off evil spirits during the construction of the property. Behind panels in the wall, 186 further bundles containing hair, teeth and the names of additional 16th century children were discovered. Workers removing the remains, reported hearing the sound of children playing up and down the stairs, of chills, sounds, whispers and many other unexplainable occurrences." Subsequent newspaper reports have embellished these stories, incorporating other phenomena into the ghostly repertoire; sudden temperature drops, objects moving and taps turning on and off and even that the strange sounds continued after the building was repaired. These reports say that ghostly phenomena commenced when the historic items were removed from the premises.

Zizzi [R]
53 St Peter Street, CT1 2BE
     An extremely old building (dating to about 1200), it is named Cogan House after John Cogan who acquired the property in 1626. Another occupier was three times mayor and mercer John Bygg in 1473. It is he who is said to haunt this building, standing at the top of the stairs and brushing by people. Stories also abound of the smell of rotting fish, unexplained gusts of wind and customer's children talking to a man who sits on the benches in the garden but is invisible to adults.

Maidstone

Sir Thomas Wyatt Beefeater [R]
London Road, ME16 0HG
     The ghost is said to be that of a young woman but there are no more details.

New Romney

Costa Coffee [T] *The New Inn*
37 High Street, TN28 8BW
     Renowned for its historical connections with smuggling (including a network of tunnels), the old pub sported the figure of a young lady who was found hanged here.

Rochester

Amore [R] *The Garden House restaurant*
98 High Street, ME1 1JT
A little boy had been seen sitting in the old fireplace and was blamed for items being moved around.

Cafe Nucleus and Nucleus Arts Gallery [T] *Halpern Conservancy Offices*
15 High Street, ME1 1PY
A spectral old man has been seen near the main door, in a room that previously used to be a kitchen; it is said that a man gassed himself after encountering financial problems and some believe that he is this ghost. A solid grey mass was also once seen near the stairs.

Pizza Express [R]
21-23 High Street, ME1 1LN
Sounds as if objects are being moved around have been heard in the cellar, and during refurbishment rocks and debris were flung about by an unseen hand.

The Quills [R] *Angel Energy Centre shop*
30-32 High Street, ME1 1LD
Three ghosts were said to haunt this old (c.1500) building; a little boy who runs through the building towards the rear, also a woman and a man.

Smoqe [R] *Dot Cafe*
172 High Street, ME1 1EX
The kitchen area was haunted by an unseen ghost and staff reported hearing "masculine sighs," feeling the sensation of being touched, and detecting the smell of cigarette smoke.

Sol Y Sombra [R] *Atrium restaurant*
86 High Street, ME1 1JY

The apparition of a young girl wearing a colourful dress had been observed on the stairs by the entrance door; other visible phantoms are the shadowy form of a man near the toilets and a head waiter at the top of the stairs. Other than these phantoms items would sometimes go missing in the kitchen and an ex-chef was hit on the head with a metal hanger. Also, the owner of the restaurant felt a crushing pressure when he stayed in the building overnight.

Tunbridge Wells

La Casa Vecchia [R]
70-72 The Pantiles, TN2 5TW

Although her face is never seen, a 70 year old woman in a cloak or long grey dress has been seen staring out of a first class window; it is this area where furniture had been found rearranged overnight. In addition, an ex-manager's wife was jostled on the staircase by the phantom.

In February 2020, the establishment replied to my query for any recent phenomena; "The bar upstairs is supposedly haunted by 'the grey lady.' Some of our staff members have reported feeling a presence etc .when in the bar late at night and alone." Perhaps not so coincidentally, the upstairs bar and live music venue is called "The Grey Lady."

Five Guys [R]   *Closs and Hamblin homeware*
113-115 Mount Pleasant Road TN1 1QS

Workers at the old premises believed that it was haunted. Employees talked of a presence in the basement, and they have heard voices and one of the workers felt something touch her shoulder a few times. My correspondent even said, "the staff knew the name of the ghost but has since forgotten it."

West Malling

Frank's Restaurant and Mussel Bar [R]   *The Bakery restaurant*
53-57 High Street, ME19 6QH

A phantom monk has been seen seated upstairs at a writing desk in this 15th century building.

The Hungry Guest [T]   *Mackenzie's Wine Bar*
65 High Street, ME19 6NA

A draped figure thought to be a monk was seen to walk across the bar; this may be connected to a fireplace in the building which it is claimed once belonged to the nearby Abbey (though it is also said that this fireplace dates back to the 15th century when this building and the adjoining one were conjoined and called "The Bull" inn). In the same year (1988) as this sighting, the owner's son accidentally knocked over a bucket in the kitchen but a hand appeared and prevented the contents from spilling.

London

Barnet
The Red Lion (Stonehouse Pizza and Carvery)   *The Dandy Lion/The Red Lion*
31 High Street, Chipping Barnet, EN5 5UW

The ghostly figure of a lady in grey has been seen here and it is reputed that she was either a traveller who was visiting the pub or was a barmaid. Her curiosity overwhelmed her and she went to eavesdrop on a Masonic meeting in an upstairs room but was discovered and in her efforts to escape, she fell down the stairs and died. Apart from this grey phantom, the only other story was that a punter many years ago said that as she was in the toilets, a cubicle door flew open, and she heard the sound of an "old style" toilet being flushed - even though none of the lavatories had been used.

Much later, a former manager said that while the site was being renovated, builders told him that they would see something in their peripheral vision, and that the shadows seemed to be heading towards the flight of stone stairs at the rear. The manager's Dobermann would stare at the wall separating his abode on the 3rd floor from the older areas of the pub, which were disused at the time. The manager also found the plugs for the toaster and kettle ripped with her wall forcibly; the sockets were in the partition wall that had so fascinated his dog. An employee felt that the ghost had followed her home when she saw a misty female form bending over her baby's cot. Eventually in 1986 a "cleansing" of the property was performed, when a "whoosh" went through the old ballroom and out of the door. This seemed to have been the last hurrah for the phantom as nothing more was noted after this.

Greenwich

Goddards at Greenwich [R]
22 King William Walk, SE10 9HU
 Goddards have been based here since 1952, and according to a 2024 newspaper, "Over the years staff have reported hearing the sounds of plaintive wailing in the cellar, which is believed to belong to one of the victims killed by the plague."
 In March 2025 the restaurant informed me that they "haven't collectively experienced anything" ghostly related.

Westminster:

Maroush at Crocker's Folly [R]   *Crocker's Folly*
24 Aberdeen Place, St John's Wood, NW8 8JR
 The ghost here is former landlord and owner Frank Crocker. A legend exists (which has been disproven) that Crocker killed himself in despair when a new train station was built some distance away; the story continues that he had anticipated that the building would be closer, bringing in more custom. In reality, Crocker died of natural causes after a long illness.

Oxfordshire

Burford

Nutmeg and Thyme at No31 [T]   *Old grammar school tuck shop*
31 High Street, OX18 4RN
 A disembodied hand came up through a window seat, gave "a little twirl" and then disappeared. The seat was located above the cellar but a search below found no-one present who could have perpetrated a hoax. Interestingly, the cottage next door in Church Lane has/had a similar spectral

visitation; a gloved hand once appeared through the wall next to the window seat, although there is some confusion as to whether this sighting actually occurred in the tuck shop. These phenomena would seem to be somewhat old and it is not known if there have been any recurrences lately. It also isn't clear if this ghostly hand made regular appearances or was just a "one off."

Surrey

Dorking

Kenito's Piri Piri [R]   *
5-6 New Parade, London Road RH4 1RQ
   When this was a hairdresser's salon (c.1960), a ghostly dog would sit on the stairs that led to the flat above; a visitor used to step over it as she ascended, while a former resident's cat would hiss at something that only it could see.

Mullins Coffee Shop [T]
58 West Street, RH4 1BS
   A spectre wearing a dark suit and white breeches ascends from the cellar, but as he turns to the front door, he then vanishes. The figure has been identified by some as William Mullins, who was a Pilgrim Father on the Mayflower and who lived here in the 17th century.

Farnham

Caffe Piccolo [R] *The Mitre pub
84 West Street, GU9 7EN
   A number of phantoms were (are?) in residence here; a soldier attired in a uniform from the Wellington era who has been seen guarding the entrance; additionally, the rear of the building was the "domain" of a 19th century serving girl while a phantom couple were noted on the stairs.

Guildford

Tortilla Guildford [R] *Millets outdoor accessories*
21 Friary Street, GU1 4EH
A phantom monk was seen to walk into the building from the old branch of Woolworths that was next door; he had been blamed for incidents of mischief such as knocking things to the floor, breaking items and pulling rucksacks from the wall. As one employee was locking up, she saw a man in old-fashioned clothing walk past her out of the corner of her eye. The next day, she was at the top of the stairs telling a co-worker of her experience when she saw the monk at the bottom looking up at her. Interestingly, it is in this area of the town that people gained access to the Guildford Dominican Friary.
In March 2020, the establishment told me that all was quiet at the restaurant.

West Sussex

Chichester

The Buttery at the Crypt [T]
aka "The Buttery"
12A South Street, PO19 1EJ
A playful spirit pinches the bottoms of waitresses here!
The manager told me in January 2020 that they had not had any paranormal reports in recent years although he had heard of a YouTube video which demonstrated some of the claimed activity. Much later, a customer named Mark emailed me in March 2025 and told me that c.2017 he and his wife went to a New Years event here and about 11pm he witnessed 3 or 4 glasses slide sideways off the shelf, falling to the floor with a crash. A nearby staff member was quite shocked by this incident.

The Giggling Squid [R] *The Chichester Observer newspaper*

Unicorn House, PO19 1JN

A variety of inexplicable occurrences were noted here; drawers being pulled open by themselves, doors opening and closing, a guillotine used by printers being hurled off a cabinet, computer keyboards being pressed by invisible fingers and figures being seen.

West Midlands

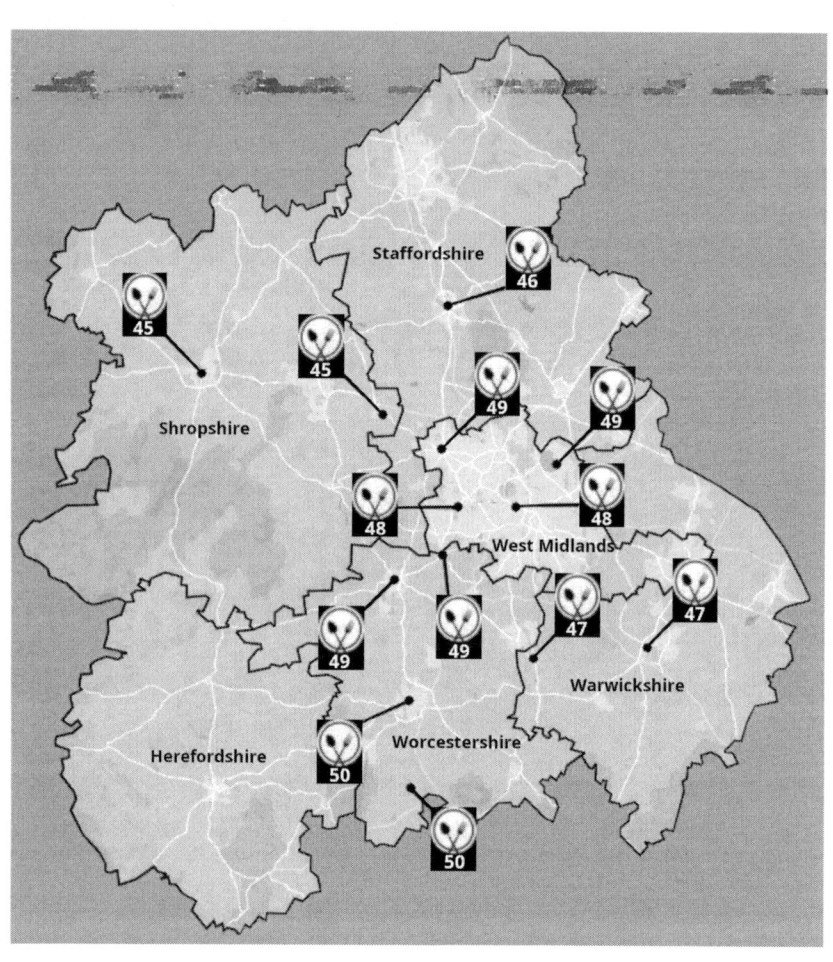

Shropshire

Albrighton

The Cowshed [R] *The Horns of Boningale*
Holyhead Road, Boningale, WV7 3DA
Three apparitions are associated with this location; a short lady sometimes described as an old maid who wipes down the tables is seen in the old dining room; a man with an unclear face and dressed in a smock, observed leaning against the mantelpiece of the dining room (latterly he was to be noted in the cellar too); and at the rear of the premises, a man in a tweed jacket who leans against the bar. It is rumoured that the man in the smock may be a drover who was murdered by a fellow after a fight in their old dormitory here. A poltergeist nicknamed "Henry" has been blamed for things being hidden from view and turning taps on in the night. His presence is heralded by an icy chill. Strange smells of sweat, tobacco and perfume have also been detected in the cellar. The cellar was also the site of an alarming encounter for one employee: she went down to replenish an ice bucket and heard a cough behind her. She turned to look at the source of this sound and saw a bottle in a crate that had been left upended, and watched it turn until it was the right way up. The employee backed off and then fled the scene! She later returned to the pub after it was renovated, and said that the atmosphere was much lighter, as if the presence had gone.

Shrewsbury

Al Piccolino [R]
9 Castle Gates, SY1 2AE
The ghost of a male usher has been seen in the shop, urging people to move along. He has sometimes been seen in the ladies toilets too!

Crafty Cat Tea Lounge and Cakery [T] *The Gallery Tearoom*
24-25 Princess Street SY1 1LW
Four children who died in a fire at 25 Princess Street in the 16th century have been seen huddled in a corner.
The previous proprietors of this property told me in March 2022 that they have always had odd things going on inside, especially during the night.

When they arrived in the morning, they would find that things have been moved.

CSONS [R]   *Poppy's Tudor Tearooms*
8 Milk Street, SY1 1SZ
Two spectral children were to be seen on the stairs, with the boy opening and closing the front door occasionally. The children's parents are also spectres here; the father has been seen smoking a pipe in a window, while the mother was located in the upper restaurant. There are/were two more ghosts here too. The first is a coachman, who wears a long coat and tall hat and whose domain was the courtyard at the rear. He was seen looking to the upper floors were a phantom maid has been observed.

In February 2020, the manager said of the ghosts, "Apparently [a] girl age approx 11 in Victorian night dress [has been] seen several times" but admitted that nothing has been experienced since the plumbing was done, over 5 years previously.

Staffordshire

Stafford

The Soup Kitchen [R]
2 Church Lane, ST16 2AW
A ghost nicknamed "Ethel" is to be seen, but it's apparel is confusing; it wears a dress but there are suggestions that this may be a misidentification of a cloak. There have been incidents of paranormal japes in the property, reminiscent of poltergeist pranks. The oven has been found switched off before reaching its preset temperature, and the coffee hot plate has also similarly been found deactivated. Plates have been observed "spinning" on the floor, unexplained noises heard upstairs, and staff have been pelted with paper cups at the top of the stairs - a similar incident happened with plastic drinks lids in the yard.

Warwickshire

Studley

The Barley Mow Steakhouse Pizza and Carvery [R]
Priory Square, B80 7BA

An Augustinian Priory was nearby and its brewhouse is thought to have occupied part of the site of the Barley Mow; consequently, some of the spectral denizens are described as monks, one of which has been given the nickname "Charlie." There have been a number of other apparitions in this supernaturally charged location. An assistant manager once said that after locking up and turning the alarm on, he saw the silhouette of a woman with long blonde hair in his doorway but when he approached her, she had gone. Customers complained that their order for coffee had not arrived but when they gave a description of their server to employees, it matched no-one working there. Other phantoms include a man and a women in conversation in the bay window; the man was aged 24, with a round face and dressed in black, in a frock coat, buckled shoes and a tricorn hat. The woman's was described as pretty but her features were not so well defined. The building is replete with other incidents. Doors with heavy latches would be found opened after they had been locked; and despite the sound of furniture moving downstairs, the alarm was never activated. A waitress was delivering a meal when she heard a voice behind her saying, "I'm watching you," but there was no-one there. A pet dog was terrified of a corridor in the building and became so nervous that the owners had to get rid of it. It is said that the time around November 5th is the most paranormally active period.

In September 2020, the pub responded to my query about any recent phenomena; "Having worked in and lived above the pub for several years now, I have heard many rumours but never experienced anything out of the ordinary I'm afraid."

Warwick

Thomas Oken Tearooms [T]
aka *The Oken Tea Rooms*
20 Castle Street, CV34 4BP

Thomas Oken, who died here in 1573, was a wool dealer and became the richest man in the town. When he passed on he left certain charitable bequests to the town. If reports are accurate he still frequents his old home in death, having been seen in the area of the stairs, where footsteps are attributed to him.

An email from the tearoom in January 2020 confirmed that they still have phantoms in residence, one of whom is identified as Oken, who "wanders around upstairs. [Another] one is the ghost of a female servant. And the third is a child (a girl) who hangs around at the bottom of the stairs. Some young women have felt a tug at their clothes as they go down the stairs - they feel that the little girl is holding something (jacks?) and wants to play." A follow-up email in March 2025 confirmed that incidents were still occurring but they now seemed to be more low-key: "We haven't got big stories, but certainly the staff have tails [tales] of footsteps on the stairs when they are along [alone] in the building, a child's laughter and someone pulling at their shirt that they can't explain ... these are all quite recent sightings and hearings."

West Midlands

Dudley

The Queen Mary [R]
Castle Hill, Dudley Zoo and Castle   DY1 4QB
A phantom pianist has been heard when the building is empty.

Birmingham

Sheldon Hall Pizza and Carvery [R]
Gressel Lane, Sheldon, B33 9US
There would seem to be two ghosts here; a young girl and an old lady. Sadly there are no more details.

Sutton Coldfield

Mitchells Shopping [T/R?] *Fox Hill*
Weeford Road,   B75 6NA
> The old "Hungry Horse Tearoom" at Fox Hill is/was the home of an elderly Edwardian lady in a pinny and headdress. On one occasion she was seen standing where the door to the backyard was originally located. It isn't known if the current "Farmhouse Bistro" restaurant occupies the same location as the old tearoom.

Wolverhampton

Roti Pani Indian Restaurant and Bar [R]
Dale House, Bilston Street, Willenhall WV13 2AW
> There is a ghost that seemed to "shimmy" across the upstairs landing.

Worcestershire

Hagley

Beefeater Badger's Sett [R]
Birmingham Road, DY9 9JS
> A ghost of a man in a tweed jacket has been seen inside this pub and in the 1970s, poltergeist-like pranks comprising of lights going on and off, doors opening and closing and items moving by themselves would occur.

Kidderminster

Kidderminster Fish Bar [R] *Corn Exchange pub*
95 New Road, DY10 1AF
> An elderly woman in a cream suit, dating to the 1970s was once seen standing by a column; locals claim that she was a previous landlady named "Mary" and has also been observed on the top floors too. A tall dark haired

man in Edwardian clothes who walked across the bar downstairs after closing time is another apparition. "Something" was also seen in a first floor bedroom but details are absent. Lightbulbs blowing, and telephones and the jukebox malfunctioning have also occurred in the pub. Meanwhile licensees had reported items going missing and reappearing in other, odd locations in the upstairs area. The pub also had an effect on the landlord's pets; the dog wouldn't go down the stairs at night and two cats suffered from such personality changes in the pub that they had to be rehomed

Upton upon Severn

Pundit's Fusion [R] *Amigos Restaurant*
9 Old Street, WR8 0HN
  A number of phenomena have occurred in the past, but the only visible apparition was described as having an injured eye and wearing a leather jacket and a roughly stitched white shirt with a frill. Additionally there were tapping noises coming from a table reminiscent of a Civil War drum beat, the restaurant owner being poked in the back while in bed at night, "red stars" being seen upstairs, the washing machine malfunctioning (nothing could be found amiss with it) and the owner's dog becoming so agitated by something that it tried to flee the premises.

Worcester

Cafe Piano [R] *The Bottles Wine Bar*
5 Friar Street, WR1 2LZ
  During the 1990s, a host of odd incidents plagued the staff here. An employee who mopped the floor at the end of the evening would return to her work to find buckets moved from behind the bar to the middle of the floor, and no footprints were seen in the damp floor; this same member of staff would find herself trapped in the cellar when a crate of bottles were moved. Footsteps were heard ascending the stairs and walking along the balcony after new refrigerators were fitted. A cask was seen to fall over, roll and then right itself, and a stack of pans was found to have been moved during the night, but this movement hadn't triggered the burglar alarms. There had been problems with electrical items (including the heating system, CD player and lights), candles going out and people hearing bizarre sounds (a howl heard while going up to the balcony, and a short female scream in the yard).

Note: when *Cafe Rouge* occupied the premises some years later, the management were hostile to investigations and chats with staff that mentioned ghosts. One researcher was reportedly "thrown out" for asking about any current reports.

Toby Carvery Worcester West   [R]   *The Ketch Inn/Toby Carvery Worcester West*
Bath Road, WR5 3HW
        The ghost was nicknamed "Olive" and had a penchant for turning lights on and off, bending cutlery, throwing a guest's belongings around his room, and opening the bar windows during the night. She is said to "live" in the cellar, where pumps had been found turned off; furthermore, the owner's dog refused to venture down there.
        The general manager replied to my query about recent phenomena when I contacted her in February 2020. She had lived here for 7 years previously, apparently without incident but everything changed in 2017. In that year she moved into a previously unused bedroom which provoked incidents such as night terrors. As she said, "on numerous occasions I appeared to have injured myself in my sleep (cuts/stab wounds/black eyes). Once I checked the CCTV and I left the pub through a fire exit at 3am and went into the bunker under the pub. I woke up in bed with a black eye at 7am but on CCTV there was no sign of me returning to bed. That summer I also smashed all of the windows in that room in my sleep. I stopped using the room after that instance as something seemed off." A lady who visited the pub in 2019 told my correspondent that she used to live in the pub and that the afflicted bedroom had been boarded up as people were becoming "possessed." As I was told, "Once I stopped using that room the issues stopped. Just a few weeks ago (i.e. late 2019/early 2020) somebody stayed in that room for a few nights, and I've had strange things happening again since, including another sleep injury despite not having one for over a year." The room was then blocked off. My contact concluded, "There are also strange noises [and] there is a bunker under the pub, and somebody bangs on the ceiling and you can hear and feel it when stood behind the bar. The area that the banging occurs is no longer accessible."

East Midlands

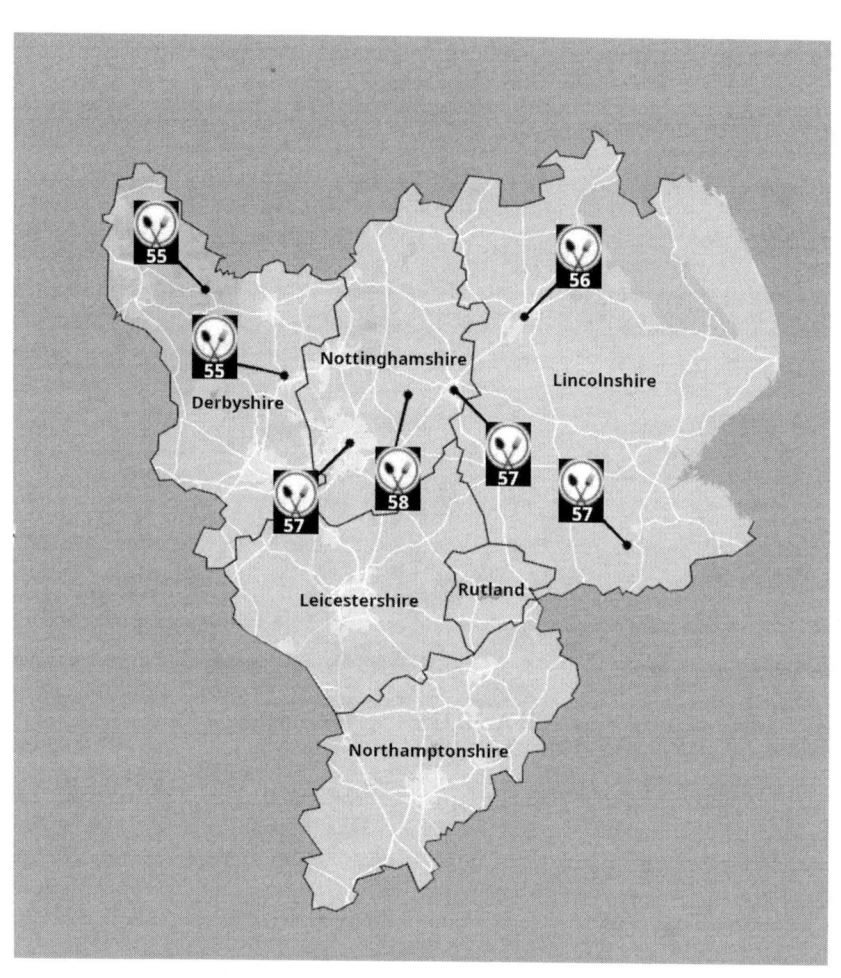

Derbyshire

Alfreton

Alfreton House [T]
127 High Street, DE55 7HH

Phantom footsteps have occurred in this 17th century building, and on a few occasions, a pile of baby clothes left in a locked room was found to have been rifled through.

Pesto at the Peacock [R] *The Peacock Hotel*
1 Chesterfield Road, Fourlane Ends, DE55 7LN

The most famous phantom here is Dick Turpin (a most ubiquitous ghosts, as he has been seen in many other locations in the UK!). He is reputed to have been seen most notably in the car park where the stables were located and where his steed Black Bess was supposedly concealed (even though this story is on historically dubious grounds). The other apparition is a monk without a face. He wears a white gown and is seen hovering above the ground.

Stoney Middleton

Curry Cottage at Lovers Leap [R] *Lover's Leap Inn*
The Dale, S32 4TF

In 1762, Hannah Baddalay (or Baddaley) was courting William Barnsley, but when he broke off their relationship she threw herself off the cliffs; however, her skirts acted like a parachute and broke her fall. She died two years later, some say of natural causes while other people say due to injuries incurred her fall (though most versions of this tale say that she only suffered minor cuts and bruises). Hannah's ghost is said to re-enact her suicide bid.

The restaurant management informed me in January 2020 that, in their five years of occupancy, nothing has been experienced.

Lincolnshire

Lincoln

Hobbsons Restaurant and Pie Shop [R] *Browns Pie Shop
33 Steep Hill, LN2 1LU

This building might date as far back as the 14th century and has fronted a variety of businesses including a pub, bookshop, and an antiques shop before becoming Brown's Pie Shop in 1987. In its previous guises, a famous resident was Lawrence of Arabia in 1925. The premises were/are home to a spectre named "Humphrey" who is/was said to inhabit the first floor kitchen and has been described as a young boy aged about 8 years old. Staff were said to greet him with a friendly "Good Morning" to placate him when they arrived. On one occasion, a temporary chef, who did not know of the customary salutation, returned to his counter to find a knife that he had just been using embedded in the floor; it was said to have been thrown with considerable force as it was still quivering. Humphrey has also been blamed for footsteps, items moving and being thrown about (such as a fire blanket that was hurled at the chef), lights turning on and off, coins levitating before falling to the ground with a clatter, the front door slamming shut (the keys being thrown to the ground) and interference with ingredients. Away from his customary domain, there were suspicions of some form of paranormal activity on the third floor as it was unnaturally cold.

Although the establishment ignored my query for any recent phenomena in 2020, the manager of Brown's gave an interview to the press in December 2021 where he recounted some of the incidents mentioned above. Lots of people, both customers and employees have experienced things, and CCTV had caught objects moving unaided. The owner said that his children were "always looking around and talking to [Humphrey]."

The Jews House Restaurant [R]
15 The Strait, LN2 1JD

This building dates back to the 12th century and was part of the thriving Jewish community in England, until they were expelled from England in 1290. A former resident of this building was Belaset, daughter of Solomon of Wallingford. She was hanged in 1287 when she was convicted of clipping coins. Whether she was responsible for the reports of footsteps and bumping noises, the sounds of doors creaking (even where there were no doors), and pots and pans moving is not known.

In June 2022 the restaurant informed me that they had not had any odd experiences at the premises since there was a fire here in 2006; they thought that this had "cleansed the building." This lack of activity was confirmed in March 2025 (although in this case they stated that the fire was in 2010).

Spalding

Katana Japanese Restaurant [R] *Spalding Fire Station/Joe's Restaurant*
42 Double Street, PE11 2AB
    Occurrences date back to the time that this building hosted the town's old fire station. The recreation room was said to be very cold and a snooker ball was found inexplicably placed on the floor; it is in this room that a carpenter committed suicide some years previously. Events seemed to escalate when the building was repurposed as a restaurant. Apparitions consisted of a dark figure in the kitchen and a spectre in the store room. Additionally, a large ball of light flew into an employee in the kitchen, wine glasses were knocked off the shelf one by one, objects moved unassisted and electrical items being interfered with occurred here. Staff had heard voices and even their names called out, sometimes quite loudly, but their colleagues have heard nothing and denied being the source of the calls even when their voices have been recognised.

Nottinghamshire

Newark-on-Trent

The Governers House [T] *
23 Stodman Street, NG24 1AW
    In the 1990s, it is said that the smell of violets in this building and the sound of footsteps in the attic were experienced.

Nottingham

Riverside Farm [R]

Tottle Road, NG2 1RT

The building is situated on the site of an old manor house, dating back over a century according to the old Greene King Website. A ghost, thought to be that of a young woman, has been seen walking from one side of the play area to the other, while elsewhere in the accommodation area, children's voices have been heard and doors open by themselves. It is also upstairs where the smell of fresh fish has been noted moving from room to room before vanishing.

Southwell

Lasani [R] *Bramley Apple Inn*
51 Church Street, NG25 0HQ

In a familiar story that is endemic to many pubs and restaurants, the taps to the pumps in the cellar are turned off by some mischievous force.

East of England

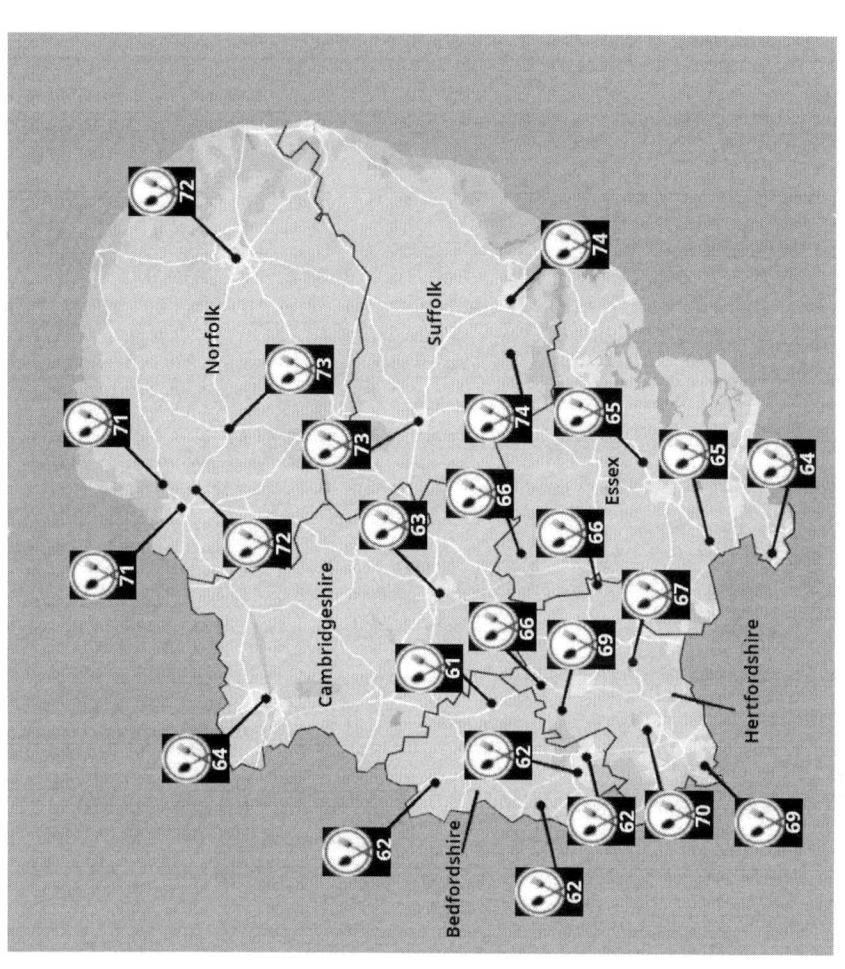

Bedfordshire

Biggleswade

Jones' Cafe [T] *Furniture Shop/Pound Stretcher/Jones*
15A High Street SG18 0JE

Previously, there had been a multitude of activity here. Mentions in the literature and research by *The Weird in the Wade* podcast team have compiled the following reports, most of them when the premises was a furniture store or a branch of Pound Stretcher: these anecdotes comprise doors shutting and windows closing on hot days, the alarm activating during the night, a man being sealed in an upstairs room (as if the door was locked), lights turning on in the men's toilets, noises coming from the unoccupied attic, stock flying around and falling on employees heads, a sensation of coldness and items found scattered when staff unlocked in the morning. These were blamed on a ghost called "Aggie," who might have been the unidentified figure of a young girl seen on the back steps.

Today, the establishment is a gymnasium, with a cafe occupying a portion of the premises. In August 2021, the cafe replied to my query for any recent phenomena saying that they had no stories to relate. In March 2025, a follow-up email was sent with slightly more encouraging results; "My colleague who has a clinic for sports physio has given me a couple things she has experienced. One being that when she is on her own sometimes in the clinic, it sounds like a ball is being bounced on her desk. And when she has been in the studio doing a stretch class, one of the benches popped off the hook that they are hung on but no one had touched it. Another colleague of mine has said that when she was closing up the cafe, she turned a light off, it stayed on and flickered. [She] turned it on and stayed on normally and then turned it off again and it did the same flickering thing. They had to keep doing it until it eventually turned off." The podcast team, a short while later, managed to elicit a few more tales. The gym manager said that there had been "a couple of things" but "nothing exciting." She had seen punchbags in the gym swaying; sometimes a few and sometimes just a random one. She had also been in the gym when she thought someone had come in, but there was no-one present. She also told how someone had been tapped on the shoulder. With regards to the cafe, staff would come in in the morning to find the coffee dispensed into piles. They had also experienced cups coming off the machine and ending up on the floor, and a knife went missing after its user had turned away briefly. A toilet light, activated by a sensor, would activate spontaneously. Another employee told how when he went into the building at

6am to open up, he saw a large dark figure (showing a "head of hair") glide across a glass pane in the cafe area.

Houghton Regis

The Chequers Hungry Horse [R]
East End, LU5 5LB
A few people who worked here have claimed that "odd things" have happened. A group of cleaners, who had taken a brief respite from their toil, noticed a door nearby slightly, and then one of them was yanked off the chair by an invisible force. There is also said to be a dark shadowy figure in the premises and CCTV footage has caught glasses falling off the shelves after closing time.

Luton

The Old Moat House [R]
Moat Lane, LU3 1UU
A veiled woman, believed to be a nun, has been seen here, and a figure has been observed going down into the cellar. Elsewhere, lights switch on and off in empty parts of the building.

Sharnbrook

The Spice Tree [R]   *The Fordham Arms pub*
Templars Way, MK44 1PX
The only report of an apparition was of a shadowy figure wearing a cape that was seen to "flit" across the bar and disappear into the wall where a door used to be. Other than this, the only other report was of a plastic scoop that "whizzed" past the ear of the landlord in the cellar.

Woburn

Fratelli Cucina Italiana [R]   *The Royal Oak*

40 George Street, MK17 9PY

Dating back to the 1600s, this building might have comprised three structures but by 1774 it had become an inn, a guise it maintained until it became a restaurant in 2016. Before then, there was a large catalogue of paranormal phenomena; beer taps turning off, doors slamming, flowers taken out of vases, drinks launching off tables, beds moving and sometimes an old playing card dropping from the ceiling; one time, a tankard dropped to the floor with no explanation. The ghost was most usually connected to the stairs leading to the cellar. A local story talks of a World War 1 soldier who used to frequent the pub in death, even leaving money at the bar for a drink. An elaboration to this tale adds that the soldier had been injured in the war and did not wish his disfigurement to be seen by the townsfolk so he arranged to drink in the pub after hours when everyone else had departed. The landlord would leave a drink on the counter and the soldier would leave reimbursement behind. The tale concludes that one evening the landlord found money on the bar as usual when he went to lock up the building; he had been told that earlier on during the day the soldier had passed away.

Cambridgeshire

Cambridge

Indigo Coffee House [T]
8 St Edward's Passage CB2 3PJ

Furniture has been found piled up and other objects been found moved, including a trail of marshmallows left as a trail on the steps down to the kitchen in the cellar!

Ittou Noodle Bar [R] *Rainbow Vegetarian Cafe*
9 King's Parade, CB2 1SJ

The phantom is believed to be Sarah "Sadie" Barnet, a landlady who disciplined students when they stopped here and fell short of her standards. There had been footsteps and the sound of coughing, and a manager was pushed roughly to one side. In addition, a member of the kitchen staff saw an apparition briefly, accompanied by a lingering smell of perfume.

Little Rose [R]   *Loch Fyne Restaurant*
37 Trumpington Street,   CB2 1QY
The first wife of a Peterhouse College master haunted this building; she used to tend to the undergraduates who lodged at the old hostelry on this site.

In February 2020, the manager of Loch Fyne told me that he hadn't worked at the establishment long enough to notice anything, but his team were convinced that things like glasses that fell to the floor by themselves and smashing could be attributed to the ghost(s).

Peterborough

Prezzo Peterborough [R] *The Falcon (or unnamed pub?)/Prezzo*
2 Cowgate,   PE1 1NA
When the building was a pub (at some point prior to it becoming a restaurant in 2004), a man in Georgian attire was seen drinking a pint of beer at the bar only to vanish when people approached him. Since then, there have been mentions of another ghost, namely that of a Victorian lady with a disapproving look who has been seen looking out of the first floor window in the "turret."

Essex

Aveley

Sir Henry's Restaurant [R]
Romford Road, RM15 4XB
The restaurant's website mentions that, "It is said that late at night a headless horseman can be seen riding across the old Belhus estate to where the main gate once used to be ... When staff lock up footsteps can be heard coming from the restaurant above even though no-one is up there and a door in the main bar bangs loudly as if some is trying to get into the building. The

kitchen has also had it share of strange events. A gas burner has been found turned on in the morning and kitchen equipment never seems to stay were you put it. Paperwork always seems to go missing, glasses have jumped off of the bar area, and staff often feel breezes pass through them."

Brentwood

Harvester Golden Fleece [R]
101 London Road, CM14 4NP
01277 224511
    Patrons have noticed a phantom monk in the mirror, but when they turn around, he has vanished!

Masons [R] *The Fountain Head*
155-157 Ingrave Road, CM13 2AA
    Poltergeist-like activity has occurred here, with specific mentions of moving furniture and exploding bottle.

Hatfield Peverel

Blue Strawberry Bistrot [R]
The Street, CM3 2DW
    Phenomena here is said to be regular but the only apparition noted appeared on CCTV showing showing a white figure sitting at the bar. Bottles have fallen off shelves, the plug was pulled out of the wall when the owner's daughter was using a vacuum cleaner, waitress have felt something pulling at their aprons and the owner heard a female voice say "Hey" when he was locking up at night.
    In June 2021, the property replied to my query about recent phenomena saying, "We do have a 'ghost' [and] have pics as well" but nothing more could be ascertained despite further emails.

The William B [R]
aka "The William Boosey" and "Fish at The William Boosey"
The Street, CM3 2ET

Three phantoms are said to reside here but there are few details other than they delight in creating noises and cold spots and workers behind the bar have been pushed.

Saffron Walden

The Courtyard Tea Room [T] *Gluttons tearoom*
aka Tiptree Tea Room
2-3 Rose & Crown Walk, CB10 1JH
Electrical failures here were blamed on a poltergeist.

Hertfordshire

Baldock

Pixies [T] *Mayflower Gift Shop?/?*
24A High Street, SG7 6AX
Once a newsagent and then a sweet shop, objects being thrown and moved by themselves were blamed on the pranks of a poltergeist.

Bishop's Stortford

Baan Thitiya [R]
102 London Road, CM23 3DS
Heralded by brightly coloured butterflies in the summertime, a "gaudy coloured" old lady haunts the garden.

Caffe Nero [T] *Alliance and Leicester Bank*
28-32 Potter Street, Bishop's Stortford, Hertfordshire CM23 3UL
Items would be moved, the front door would be found closed, wallpaper was discovered ripped and scratches (with claw marks left behind),

an office chair skidded across the floor, and other phenomena were experienced here but further details are fragmentary.

Cote Brasserie [R] *Pearsons
17 North Street, CM23 2LD

When these premises was a department store that sold handbags, a grey misty female figure haunted the cellar.

In March 2020, the manager informed me that they were yet to notice anything odd in the restaurant.

Prezzo [R] *The George
1 North Street, CM23 2LD

This building and the hotel next door used to operate under the name of *The George*, but when a portion was converted into a restaurant, the remainder around the corner retained its name and function as guest accommodation. The portion that was a pub had the apparition of a spectral man in the cellar and beer taps were manipulated by unseen hands; this area is now part of the toilets.

Sabrosa Del Fuego [R] *The Boar's Head
30 High Street, CM23 2LX

Bishop's Stortford perennial phantom, "The Grey Lady," has been claimed for this location (or at least, walking past on her way to the church opposite), but a multitude of other incidents have been reported inside; inexplicable bangs at the front door, the smell of burning, optics and waste bins shaking, glasses and bottles hurled off off shelves, chairs being dragged by something invisible and a credit card machine going haywire were reported. All these incidents have occurred since an exorcism, obviously unsuccessful, many years ago.

Hertford

Brew Garden [T] *Monsoon Accessorize
3 Maidenhead Street, SG14 1DP

Footsteps and the sound of someone using a vacuum cleaner had been heard originating from an (at the time) unused area in the upstairs portion of the building.

The Golden Dragon [R]   *The Three Tuns pub*
34 St Andrew Street, SG14 1JA

A number of phenomena had been observed here, the most intriguing being a "bedraggled" young girl who walked through a wall and then up a non-existent staircase. Objects moving (such as glasses jumping off the shelves) and items going missing were reported here, especially in the back area near the ladies' toilets

No 5 Eat and Drink [R]   *?/Perrins/No 5 Eat and Drink*
5 Old Cross, SG14 1HX

When this building was a clothes shop, clothing in the basement would billow as if blown by a breeze, tobacco would be smelt, trainers would move, the sound of something moving would be heard and a dark shadow was seen. A figure was followed into the stockroom, but no one was there upon investigation, and the sensation of a small dog jumping up and clawing at the proprietor's leg was felt.

The current owners of the property told me in April 2025 that they have had "loads of activities" (which makes these premises a rarity - a location where activity has persisted after a change in name or function). The restaurant provided a few snippets of CCTV footage; the first segment came from the time that the property was a barbers (probably *Perrins*) and showed a brief flash in the corner and a drawer opening by itself. In the second piece of footage (taken on March 21st of that year) the top of a cocktail shaker on the counter spun by itself.

Pizza Express [R]   *Dimsdale Arms/Pizza Express*
80 Fore Street, SG14 1BY

While being converted from a pub, workers fled the building due to 'something' in the cellars. The restaurant apparently has had tales of items mysteriously moving.

Ruay Rot [R]   *Wigginton's Toy Store*
6 Old Cross, SG14 1RB

The ghostly Victorian lady from Leaf (at No.8 next door and currently closed at the time of writing) was seen here and stroked the brow of the owner's daughter, waking her up as she lay in bed. There were also stories of a man from the same era, described as having white hair and beard and was wearing a mourning suit.

The occupiers of 6 Old Cross in March 2020 (Galos UK) informed me that as far as they were aware, nothing has been experienced recently.

Hitchin

Esquires Coffee [T] *Charisma Beads*
8 Market Place, SG5 1DR
Staff had been "pelted" by beads and the shop's lights had been known to come on by themselves in the night

Halsey's Deli and Eatery [R]
9-11 Market Place, SG5 1DS
The building dates back to Tudor times and the ghost here is thought to be Martha Hunt, the owner of a hat shop that occupied the site in Victorian times. Reported incidents talk of a row of tins sequentially falling from a shelf, and the contents of a pan spilling, falling in a triangular configuration.

The proprietor replied to my query in September 2020 asking about any recent phenomena, saying that in her 6 years of ownership nothing had happened. Things were still quiet in a follow-up email in March 2025; "although we in theory have a resident ghost, we have no experience of any odd happenings."

Starbucks [T] *The Tea and Coffee House*
6-7 Market Place, SG5 1DR
A ghost nicknamed "Mary Jane" was responsible for footsteps heard on the upper floors, slamming doors and moving and hiding bottles of sauce. The ghost was even adept at mimicking the manager's voice.

Rickmansworth

Miller and Carter [R] *Scotsbridge Mill*
Park Road, WD3 1AT
The ghosts were said to have "moaned, groaned and made objects appear and disappear" when there were plans to convert the old Scotsbridge Mill into a restaurant of the same name in the late 1980s; in the preceding

decade, workers mentioned the sound of footsteps and coughing, keys going missing, and the smell of perfume here. There were also tales of a headless horseman in the grounds, and the ghost of a man who murdered a girl here. Eventually, so the local rumours say, an exorcism was performed here.

In August 2020 staff stated that they had not experienced any odd phenomena here.

St Albans

Harvester Ancient Briton [R]
46 Harpenden Road, Beech Bottom, AL3 5AH
In its previous incarnation as a pub of the same name, the "shadowy" form of a woman was seen "floating around the building," while in the cellar there were reports of a gasping sound.

Shaken Cow [T] *Fisks department store*
17 High Street, AL3 4EH
Although a date on the building declares 1665, the building hails from the 15th century and was a medieval lock-up, with shops on the ground floor and storage and work space on the upper floors. In later years it was the boot and shoe shop for Fisks department store and narrowly escaped demolition in 1910. It is from this era that the ghostly tales originate, as the St Albans museum website tells us; "Number 17 is alleged to be haunted by a ghost known as 'the corset maker'. She is said to be the daughter of a manager of Fisks who kept her locked in her room when she fell in love with one of the storemen. In her distress she committed suicide. After her death a table of wedding veils in the shop was often found disturbed and some of the shop assistants saw her figure in the Abbey gardens. She is also said to haunt the basement and has been heard upstairs."

Thai Square [R] *The Tudor Tavern pub*
26A-28 George Street, AL3 4ES
Dating to the 1400s, this structure has previously been known as the Swan and Kings Head and was also an antiques shop. As The Tudor Tavern, during the clean-up period following time being called, employees would see a shadow which even chased a customer out of the building! A more recognisable phantom, given the nickname "Harry" is that of a man with a neck ruff and black tunic, seen seated at a table with a drink in front of him.

He had been blamed for poltergeist-like activity and interference with electrical equipment and switches.

The Waffle House [R] *Kingsbury Watermill*
Kingsbury Watermill, St Michael's Street, AL3 4SJ
  The voice of a spectral singing miller had been heard at the old 16th century watermill, which has been a restaurant since 1978.

Norfolk

Castle Rising

Castle Rising Tearoom [T]
School Road, PE31 6AF
  Employees would often hear the sound of chairs moving above them on the first floor and thinking that customers might want attention, they went up but found no-one there. A little girl who has been seen on this floor also seemingly has a liking for "sparkly" things and the crystals on the chandelier would often be found played with. Poltergeist-like phenomena had been encountered, such as the coffee machines obligingly being turned on when staff arrived in the morning. Apart from the girl, additional apparitions include a face peering out on the other side of the entrance window, and in the garden a transparent hooded man in a cloak. However, since the visit of a ghost hunting group some 10-15 years ago all is now quiet, except for occasional sightings of the little girl through the upstairs window; interestingly she is only ever seen from outside the building and one time, a small handprint was found on the window, resisting attempts to be washed off.

King's Lynn

Marriott's Warehouse [R] *The Green Quay/Marriott's Warehouse*
South Quay, PE30 5DT

Dating back to about 1580, archaeological findings suggest that this building once stood on an island, reached by a causeway. The most common phenomena encountered here has been the sight or smell of smoke, but the impressive catalogue of incidents include creaks and footsteps on the middle floor, the sound of chatting, a female voice saying "Ha ha ha," and another voice telling a worker not to come down to the cellar. Another strange voice was connected to a door that stubbornly refused to open; when the employee asked if anyone was inside, a voice answered "Yes" but when entry was achieved, there was no-one in there and no explanation as to why the door wouldn't open. A few guests who attended an engagement party encountered a mysterious mist, a feeling of dread and a sensation as if someone wanted to push them down the stairs. A few of the guests saw a figure on the stairs, swishing a cloak. He seemed to be displeased at their presence in the building and watched as they departed.

Pizza Express [R]
1 Saturday Market Place,   PE30 5DQ

Behind the 18th century facade is a building that houses two archways, thought to belong to a much older merchant's house. Staff have reported their cleaning cloths moved, voices whispered from vacant areas, and things flying off shelves in the washing-up area. One employee reported his name being called out and thinking it was a colleague, he asked them what they wanted, to be told they hadn't said anything.

Middleton

Middletons [R]   *The Crown*
Lynn Road, PE32 1RH

This building was a coaching inn at least as far back as 1789 and it is said that during that period a coach crushed and killed a boy. In the 1970s as "The Crown," people who were stopping at this pub reported feelings of an icy cold wind on their foreheads in the night, and the sensation of being suffocated. A more recent landlord has talked of a "whirlwind" in their living quarters and doors banging. There were also problems with gas supplies to the pumps being turned off, and a box of beer and beer kegs being moved of their own accord.

Norwich

Zak's Waterside Grill and Bar [R]
Barrack Street, NR3 1TS
     This building once housed a waterside mortuary, and while all of the phenomena today occurs in the old boathouse (and not used by the public), there have been a number of incidents over the years. Staff have heard their name called while alone, and they also report items being moved, things falling off shelves, a jug exploding on a shelf and even one sighting of a man with a top hat and shiny shoes, apparently in Victorian garb, close to the building (though there are tales of things being seen out of the corner of the eye).

Swaffham

Tutankhamun's Emporium [R]
46 Market Place, PE37 7QH
     As of January 2023, the manageress informed me that staff and customers experience phenomena quite regularly, usually about once a month. There are three apparitions here; "Nancy" a lady from the 17th or 18th century; "The Thin Man," who wears a stovepipe hat and is seen at the top of the stairs; and a "Downton Abbey"-style butler. Poltergeist-like incidents have also occurred; cold spots, which would seemingly come and go; telephones malfunctioning and lights tripping; footsteps heard downstairs when there was no-one present; and the smell of lavender and tobacco smoke. Staff would also come in in the morning and find that things had been moved overnight; as an example, they once found a box of 50 champagne glasses on the other side of the room to its original location, its contents smashed; and a painting of cat by the manageress's husband would sometimes be found face up on a nearby table-top.

Suffolk

Bury St Edmunds

Five Angel Hill Wine and Coffee House [T] *Scandinavia Coffee House*
5 Angel Hill, IP33 1UZ
On several occasions, the ghost of a young girl had been seen in the stockroom, standing in the same spot, "smiling slightly" before vanishing.

Sakura [R] *
Cupola House, 7 The Traverse, IP33 1BJ
Built in 1693, one of its famous residents is said to have been Daniel Defoe. Of its otherworldly inhabitants, the most notable is *The Brown Monk* in the cellar, who has been claimed for quite a few locations in Bury St Edmunds. It is also in the cellar that a child was heard coughing and something interfered with the beer supply – and a female phantom was encountered (she has also been seen seated at the corner of the upstairs bar). The staircase seems to be one of the epicentres of activity; feet have been seen ascending; a chill has been felt in the area; a lady dressed in white (possibly from the Victorian era) was observed on the lowest part and only visible to the barman; and an employee felt as if she had walked through a presence on the first floor level - she got the impression that the invisible entity was female. Other than these stories, there have been a number of incidents; a strange light was seen on the top floor, where the sounds of furniture being rearranged was heard; footsteps; chairs and other items being knocked over and moved; and many more.

Hadleigh

The Flying Guardsman
66 High Street, IP7 5EF
Paranormal pranks have been played here, one of which was a glass flying off a table which smashed on the floor; this prompted the landlady to tell patrons not to worry about it as strange things had happened before! The proprietors have since said that that people have seen items move by themselves, or seen something odd or heard strange sounds. Examples of incidents comprise a child's buggy rocking by itself and a glass that slid off the table and into a customer's lap.

Ipswich

The Grill At Twenty5 [R]   *Butts Wine Bar/Keo Bar Bistro (?)*
33-37 St Nicholas Street,   IP1 1TW
     In the past, there was mention of a ghost "similar" to the one at No.25 (which is currently closed but is planned to re-open in mid October 2025 as a new café-bistro) being encountered. Literature talked of a shadowy form at 25 identified as a "gentlemanly ghost" who helpfully opened and closed the door to the men's toilets on one occasion. Could it perhaps be the same phantom in both buildings (queries about any spectres in the two properties in numbers 27-31 went unanswered)?
     As of March 2025, employees at "*The Grill At Twenty5*" said that they had only been here for a few months and they had experienced nothing.
     NB: There would also be some confusion here as *Butts/Keo* (Nos.33-37) was said to be "next door" to No.25 (then called *Galley* restaurant) which, based on the street numbers, is obviously incorrect. Is it possible that *Butts/Keo* later moved up the street, like *The Grill At Twenty5*, or more likely, there is an error in the original data?

Pickwick's Coffee House [T]
1 Dial Lane, IP1 1DJ
     Once the home to Thomas Wolsey's secretary, this 15th century building is apparently home to a ghost, but staff are reluctant to discuss it.

Yorkshire and the Humber

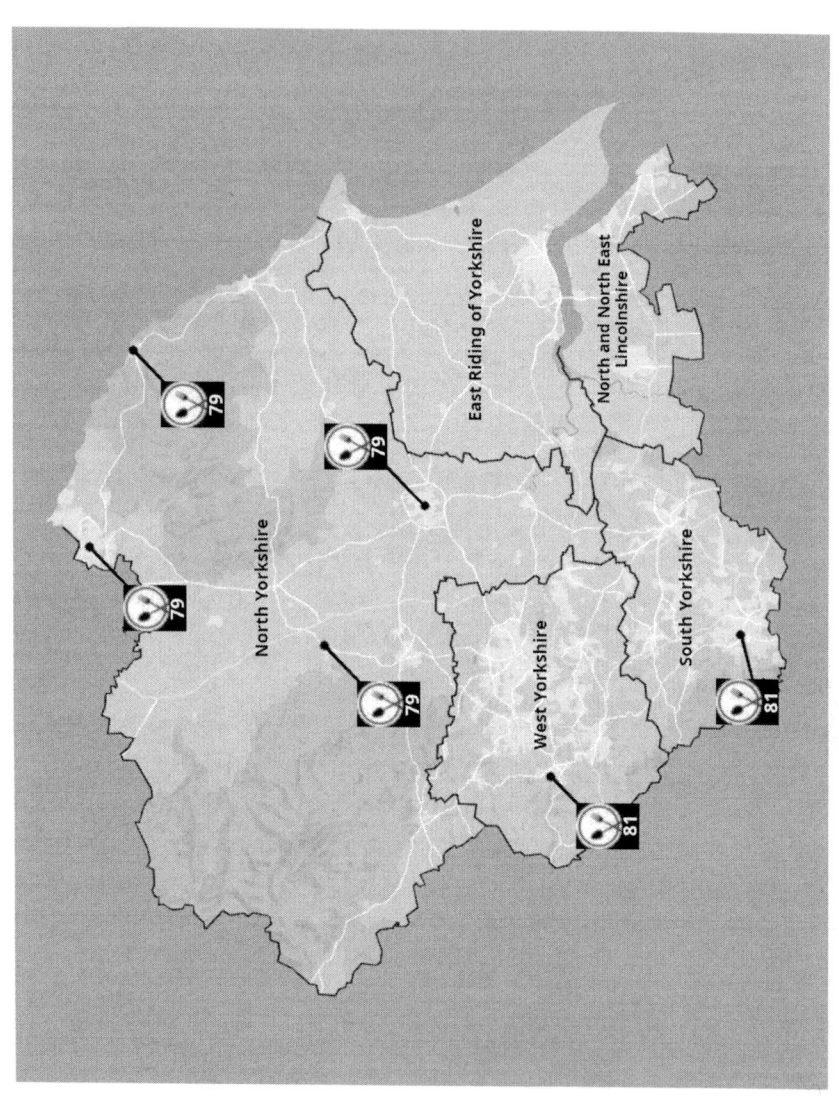

North Yorkshire

Middlesbrough

Coco and Rum [R] *TS One*
200 Linthorpe Road, TS1 3RF
"Molly the cat" was a regular spectral visitor to the old bar, and while it was never seen customers mentioned feeling the sensation of the animal in their laps and hearing purring noises.

Ripon

The Wakeman's House [T]
33 Market Place East, HG4 1BZ
The building dates from the 16th or early 17th century although most of it has been demolished since then. It is thought that Hugh Ripley lived here but there is no proof of this; the building gets its name from Ripley's role as the town's last "Wakeman" who was responsible for overseeing the security of the area during the night. When the role of Wakeman was abolished, Ripley became the town's first mayor. Regardless of the house's tenuous connection with Ripley, a figure clad in white that has been seen here is reputed to be him. Footsteps have also been heard and a row of chairs that would have blocked the path of the phantom were found moved the next day.

Whitby

Abbey Wharf [R]   *The Shambles Bar and Restaurant*
Market Place, YO22 4DD
A man who died in a fire in the building on the site prior to the Shambles is said to return as a phantom.

In August 2020, the current occupiers told me that they knew of nothing paranormal on-site.

York

The Earl Grey Tearooms [T]
13-14 The Shambles, YO1 7LZ

A visitor tried to open the toilet door but it felt as though someone was on the other side, holding it shut. When she checked back a few minutes later, the door opened unhindered and the toilet was empty. It was also here that another visitor felt the hands of a ghostly child grab her leg while she washed her hands. Employees have heard stories of a woman who "stalks" the upstairs room and an old man sitting at the corner table on the ground floor.

La Piazza Antica [R] *Marmaduke's Restaurant*
45 Goodramgate, YO1 7LS

The ghost is said to be Marmaduke Buckle who lived here 300 ago. He was severely handicapped (some say that he was deformed) and as a consequence was accused of witchcraft. The legend continues that he tried to help his family but was seen as a burden by them. Marmaduke allegedly engraved his name, year of birth (1697) and death (1715) on the wall in a 1st floor room before hanging himself from a beam here. His ghost was said to haunt this establishment, where he helpfully cleared away items.

The new owners told me in February 2025 that they had only been operating for two years in the property and in that time, nothing unusual had been experienced.

The Whippet Inn [R] *The Yorkshire Hussar*
15 North Street, YO1 6JD

The building dates back to 1896 and was home to the phantom of a man in black with a cape "slung over his shoulder" and who once walked through a wall where a bricked up doorway was located.

Unfortunately, the restaurant replied to my message in December 2021, saying that apart from a "Few creaking in doors now and then" in eight years they had experienced nothing.

South Yorkshire

Sheffield

Starbucks [T]
Carbrook Hall, Carbrook Hall Road, S9 2FJ

Sir John Bright, who built this hall, is one of the ghosts here, as is John Blunt, who owned it in the 1900s (during this period most of it was demolished and the hall became an inn). There is also said to be "an elderly woman adorned in 1920s attire," who is seen rocking in a chair. Employees at Starbucks are said to have heard the laughter of children and a baby crying as they prepare to close up the branch at night. The women's toilets are also said to have some phenomena too, where ladies have found that they were temporarily sealed into the cubicles!

West Yorkshire

Halifax

Babar Khan [R] *Design House Restaurant*
Bowling Mill, Old Lane Gate 5, Dean Clough HX3 5AX

A spectral boy of about 7 years of age had been seen (for instance in a mirror that went towards the toilet). There is also a ghostly girl; these two children were blamed for mischief like breaking glasses and interference with electrical equipment.

The North West

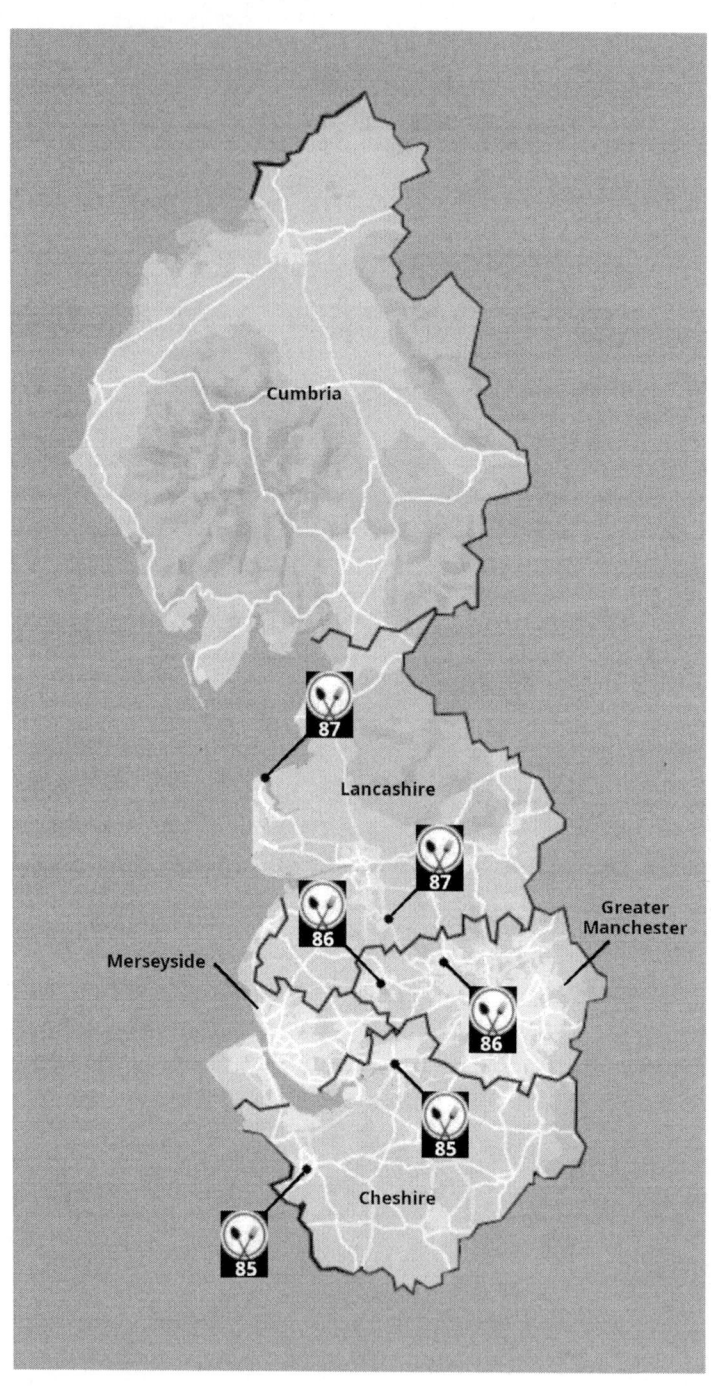

Cheshire

Chester

The Blue Bell [R]
65 Northgate Street, CH1 2HQ

The last remaining part of 12th century Lorimers Row (now long gone), this establishment has been serving alcohol since 1494. It also has a ghost that dates back to antiquity, as the website says, "The Bluebell is host to a resident ghost, Henrietta. During the English Civil War the Bluebell was used by Loyalist forces and their families as lodgings, and the cellars to stockpile grain and other provisions, keeping them safe from bombardment. So it was on September 12th 1645 that a cavalier rode off to fight in the battle of Rowton Moor, but not before bidding farewell to his wife, or maybe lover, Henrietta, with a promise to return by 10pm that night. From the upstairs window she would have watched him and others mobilise for battle, and from this window, she would almost certainly have watched events unfold. The Royalists were soundly beaten in the field, and when it became clear that he had been killed, she rushed from the window to the cellar and took her own life. It is said that Henrietta's ghost still climbs the cellar steps to this day and walks through the upstairs restaurant to the window where in life she awaited his return. [The manager has] met one person who claims to have seen the ghost and many others that have spoken of strange sightings and eerie sounds late at night."

Chez Jules [R]
71 Northgate Street, CH1 2HQ

This building is now a French restaurant and its main ghost harkens back to the time that a fire station was located here. He is "Jack," an old fireman in a brass helmet. There is also a female ghost but she is never seen; only her heels have been heard "clicking on the cobbles" at the rear.

Warrington

Welcome Break Burtonwood [R]
Junction 8, M62, Burtonwood, WA5 3AX

This service area was built on the site of RAF Burtonwood which was used by the US Air Force. The base was sited mainly on what would become the westbound carriageway and is replaced by a warehouse. Hardly surprisingly, the phantom is that of a man attired in a pilot's uniform from World War 2. On one occasion he walked across a room, and went through a door without opening it. He is reputed to have been seen "a lot."

Greater Manchester

Bolton

Toby Carvery Bolton [R]
The Watermillock, Crompton Way, BL1 8TJ
The most frequent ghostly visitor is a lady in a long dress who walks around the upper floors and descends the stairs; she may be the White Lady who was seen at the top of the staircase by a visiting American lady. The ghost seemed to be surprised and said, "You can see me!" before promptly vanishing! Another phantom is a man in a top hat and a black cloak. There are the usual reports of the sound of footsteps and items being heard and found to have moved (usually furniture) and drops in temperature. The cellar is also a source of phantom incidents. A worker was getting changed when he saw the outline of an old lady appearing. He also saw the figure of a soldier walk through the wall; this same witness noted that the building was once used as a military hospital and mortuary.

Wigan

Gallimore's Fine Restaurant [R]
13 The Wiend, WN1 1PF
The ghost is that of Albert Winstanley who worked here but was killed in an accident on-site (possibly crushed to death under a cart?) in 1923. In August 2021 the restaurant told me that there had been recent phenomena but no more details could be obtained.

Lancashire

Chorley

Luciano's at the Millstone [R]
Bolton Road, Anderton, PR6 9HJ
A "Grey Lady" has been seen here and makes the restaurant's dog nervous to go into the back room.

Fleetwood

The Ferry Cafe [T]
14 The Esplanade, FY7 6HF
The building is haunted by a male ghost that walks across the cafe and into the ladies toilets.

The owners informed me in March 2022 that when they moved into the premises three years previously, they had heard reports but had encountered nothing that could be construed as strange or unnerving.

The North East

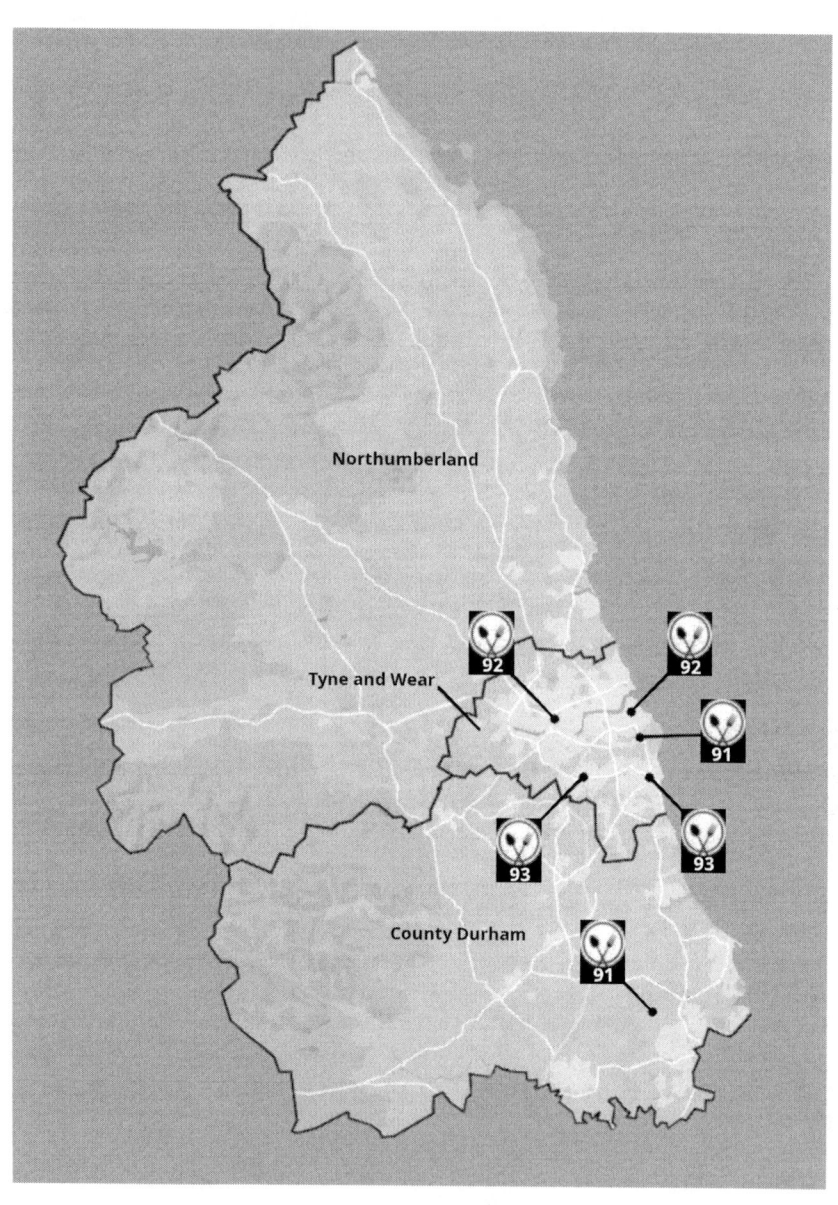

County Durham

Stockton-on-Tees

Station House Tea Rooms [T]
Wynyard Woodland Park, Wynyard, TS21 3JG

A ghost has been seen at this location, the old Thorpe Thewles Train Station. A local story tells of how the station master of nearby Wynyard Station, Mr G Dodds, discovered the dead body of his counterpart at these premises just before World War 1. He was said to have been murdered, and while no one was arrested for the crime, some Russian refugees working in the nearby woods were suspected. However, no name was given for the victim and there is no mention in the press of this incident. Further doubt arises when one finds that the station master of Thorpe Thewles, William Ormston, took up his post in November 1912 and retired in March 1922 which covers the time frame of the murder. In February 1908 James Thompson took a shortcut along the track near Thorpe Thewles and was killed when he was struck by a train. Whether he is the ghost is unknown, and there are no more details about the supposed phantom.

Tyne and Wear

Cleadon

Toby Carvery Cleadon Village [R]
Front Street, SR6 7PG

A Cavalier is fleetingly glimpsed in the corner of the bar, before he vanishes from sight; there are also stories that a Catholic Priest who fought for the Royalist cause has also been observed, and also a one-legged sailor who died on the premises in the 19th century. At least two people have seen a phantom horse and coach pass the building, with one witness adding that it actually pulled up outside and then promptly rode off again.

Newcastle-upon-Tyne

El Coto [R]
21 Leazes Park Road, NE1 4PF
    Solid shadows have been seen in the peripheral vision, but the remainder of the phenomena seem to be akin to poltergeist-like activity; auditory phenomena comprise of footsteps, knocks and tappings (in the latter case, these usually occur in a long corridor at the back of the building as if something was rapping on the windows wanting admittance) and an employee heard a voice behind him when he was alone. Among other phenomena, objects have moved unassisted and someone's trouser leg was tugged simultaneously with motion sensors activating and a drop in temperature.

El Torero [R] *
Milburn House, Side, NE1 1PR
    A spectral lady whose image appeared in one of the mirrors and the hazy figure of an old man with a walking cane was seen walking down a corridor. In addition, an employee heard her name called out in a deserted room.
    The restaurant informed me in August 2021 that when they took over the property 20 years ago the previous owner said that it was haunted by the ghost of a lady ("Mavis, I think" my correspondent said) who used to work here when it was a bank. The owner said that he had not seen anything but "There are always odd noises and funny reflections sometimes in the mirror ... I don't feel scared when I'm in on my own."

South Shields

The Hive Coffee Company [T] *Jarrow Hall*
Jarrow Hall, Church Bank, Jarrow, NE32 3DY
    The Hall was built c. 1785 by Simon Temple, the building eventually passing through the hands of various owners but is now used by the Hive Coffee Company. One of these prior owners was Isabelle Chaytor who lived here in the early 1840s and whose ghost is described as "The Grey Lady." Her ghost had been seen in the Oval Room (now a function space on the first

floor) or halfway up the stairs. Sometimes only her footsteps have been heard from downstairs. Items have also been moved around in the kitchen.

In August 2020, an employee at the coffee company told me, "As far as we are aware we haven't experienced anything out of the ordinary while we have occupied the building in afraid!" This was confirmed in an email in March 2025 when a correspondent told me, "I've worked here for about 8 years now and I'm sad to say I've never had any spooky experiences in the house!"

Log Fire Pizza Company [R] *The Railway Inn
9-11 Mill Dam, NE33 1EA

The pub was supposedly haunted by a landlady who loved it so much that she was allowed to manage it until she died. She had been seen and was known to tug the hair of people with whom she is displeased. On one occasion an unexplained icy gust was felt by a joiner working in the building.

Sunderland

Costa Coffee [T] *The Rabbie Burns pub
71 Newbottle Street, Houghton le Spring, DH4 4AR

A gruesome ghost is said to be Thomas Caldwell whose head was crushed by a beer barrel in the cellar during delivery. Other ghostly figures are of a child in Victorian clothing, and a woman whose ghostly form melted into a wall. The usual plethora of incidents (strange noises and problems with electrical equipment) have been recorded too.

Washington

The Forge [R] *The Blacksmith's Table/The Forge
The Avenue, NE38 7AB

The ghost is that of highwayman Robert Hazlitt, who was arrested at the blacksmith's shop (now the restaurant) after a local boy identified his horse from a previous crime and he alerted the authorities. Hazlitt was hanged and his corpse put in a gibbet as a warning. Other spectres include the blacksmith himself, a woman in the restaurant area who walks through the wall where the workshop used to be, and a man standing by the wall who peers over his left shoulder.

In August 2021, the proprietor of *The Forge*, who bought the property in 2017, informed me that paranormal activity was still in evidence; "We knew the stories of the highwayman, the blacksmith and the white lady from a previous owner of the blacksmiths table... he told us that if the blacksmith didn't like or agree with what we were doing the business wouldn't last long. That owner had ran his restaurant there for approximately 25 years and had seen, heard and held spiritual gatherings while he had been there. We have felt that we are certainly not alone in the building, some members of staff have seen the white lady, one member saw a dark figure behind her in the reflection in the mirror and when she turned she saw a sweeping cloak like figure disappear into the restaurant... I myself can tell when the blacksmith is around, he sits at a particular table and at the moment is quite happy with us and how we are doing things within the building. Most of the staff feel spooked when in the building on their own, I however find it OK..."

The Green [T]
The Green, NE38 7AB

The owner of the nearby *The Forge* (q.v.) informed me in August 2021 that her other premises, *The Green* tearoom was also haunted. As she said, "my mam's late husband, when helping us renovate it, often felt that he was not alone whilst working upstairs... a lady would be impatiently present... and when I was changing stock around downstairs in the shop, I knew when the young child was 'curious' about what I was doing so late at night, as I could sense I wasn't alone and there was a mischievous spirit around... some staff have known of objects moving ... on our first Christmas of 2015 in the shop, we had a late open shopping night, when everyone had gone, a few members of staff and my mam included witnessed a glass cake dome lift up from the counter and move over the other ones and then drop and smash on the floor... I knew and said straight away that the old lady had had enough noise for one night as I could sense she was annoyed. There are other little things like this but no major sightings as such." In May 2025, I contacted the tearoom to inquire about any incidents in the intervening years and was told, "the staff hear whistling right behind them sometimes and things get moved and knocked over without anyone touching them so we try to say hi and bye to the ghosts so they're in a better mood." Further correspondence revealed that these occurrences were at random but that "some people have seen a little girl as well." However no description of her, or her antics could be obtained.

Scotland

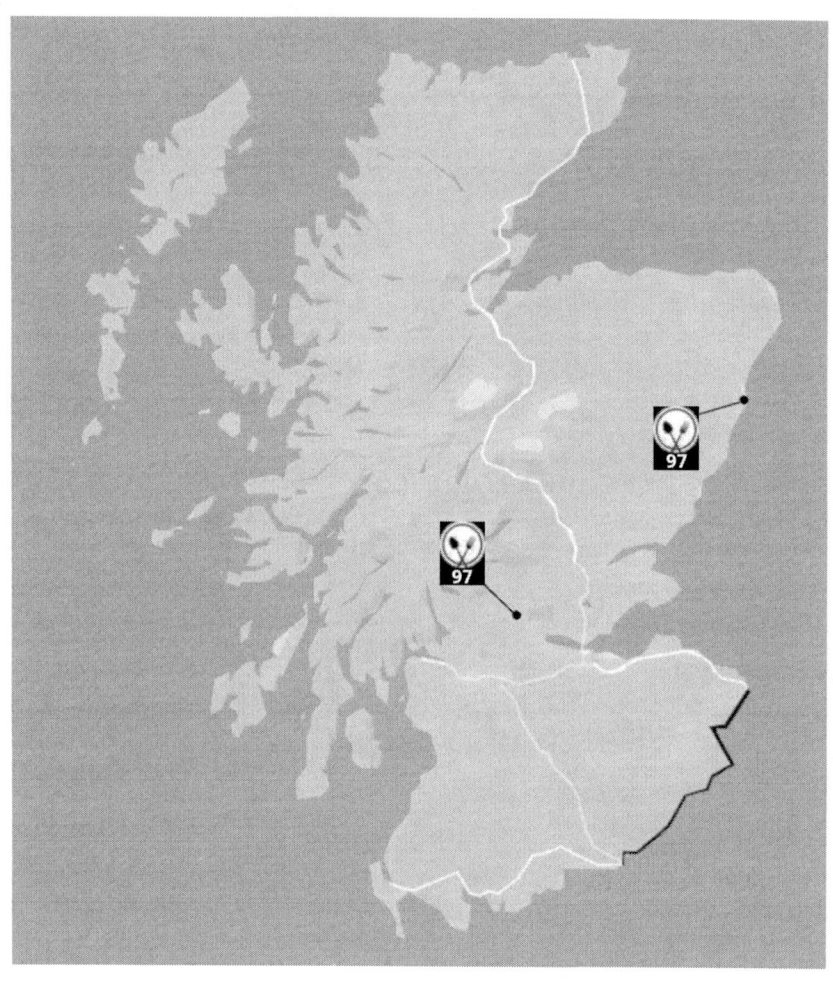

(NB: Orkneys and Shetlands and area/region names have been omitted for clarity and due to the paucity of locations)

Aberdeen

Toby Carvery Cocket Hat [R]
North Anderson Drive, AB15 6DW

The ghost is that of a previous landlord; he may also be the figure seen in peripheral vision by witnesses. Apart from this, the only other report is a "one-off" that described a whisky glass moving across a table of its own accord.

Stirling

Darnley Coffee House [T]
18 Bow Street, FK8 1BS

Doors slamming, items being swept from shelves, chairs being found to have been moved, a face peering from the entrance way and temperature drops have all been recorded here. The most terrifying incident involved someone having their shoulder squeezed as they sat on the toilet!

Printed in Dunstable, United Kingdom

71975879R00056